CHILDREN ARE CHILDREN ARE CHILDREN

CHILDREN ARE CHILDREN ARE CHILDREN

An Activity Approach to Exploring
Brazil, France, Iran, Japan, Nigeria and the U.S.S.R.

by
Ann Cole, Carolyn Haas, Elizabeth Heller,
Betty Weinberger
Illustrated by Lois Axeman

Little, Brown and Company
Boston — Toronto

By Ann Cole, Carolyn Haas and Betty Weinberger

I Saw a Purple Cow and 100 Other Recipes for Learning
(with Faith Bushnell)

A Pumpkin in a Pear Tree
Creative Ideas for Twelve Months of Holiday Fun
(with Elizabeth Heller)

FIRST EDITION

T05/78

Library of Congress Cataloging in Publication Data

Main entry under title:

Children are children are children.

  Bibliography: p.
  SUMMARY: Describes the life and customs of Nigeria,
Brazil, Japan, Iran, France, and the Soviet Union with
suggestions for related activities and projects.
    1. Manners and customs—Juvenile literature.
2. Geography—Juvenile literature. 3. Creative
activities and seatwork—Juvenile literature.
[1. Manners and customs. 2. Handicraft. 3. Cookery
I. Cole, Ann. II. Axeman, Lois.
GT85.C47   909.82'7   77-17566
ISBN 0-316-15114-9
ISBN 0-316-15113-0 pbk.

Published simultaneously in Canada
by Little, Brown & Company (Canada) Limited

PRINTED IN THE UNITED STATES OF AMERICA

ACKNOWLEDGMENTS

In researching material for *Children Are* . . . we quickly realized that it couldn't all be found in the library! It was the personal interviews and answers to our inquiries sent to acquaintances in the six countries that unearthed much of the original and colorful material which makes this book both current and unique.

We want especially to thank those people who graciously devoted valuable hours in order to share their "first-hand" experiences with us: our new *amigas* from Brazil, Clariñha Ramos, Ruth Caro and María Vidigal; Líliana McGuire, who lived in the Soviet Union for an extended period, and Janet Glenn, a student of Russian history who traveled there; Michelle Brisson Gordon and Françoise Roualt, our *amies* from France; Kaoru Sugiura and Joan Higa, Japanese-Americans; and Johangir Moini, a visitor in one of our homes, from Iran.

Our thanks also go to the many others who assisted us in providing and/or verifying particular information: Masako Okada; Reiko Katoh, English teacher in Nagoya; Theodore Welch, instructor of Japanese, Northwestern University (Japan); Annette Jaeger (France); Martha I. B. McSwain, Ph.D., Reading Specialist, Alvan Ikoku College of Education; Jill Rawnsley, a Fulbright scholar in Nigeria; Yoruba student, Aderemi Fatoke, and Hausa student Kyeri Tijani, both doctoral candidates at Northwestern University; Clara Alile, Children's Librarian, Benin City (Nigeria); Fahimeh Shanghai and Maryam Hamidi from the Iranian Consulate in Chicago and Dee Nahigian (Iran); Vivian Vallejos, translator of Portuguese (Brazil); and Barbara Bausch, elementary teacher, Amana, Iowa, who lent her expertise in many areas. *Special* thanks go to Irene Feltes, who besides typing (and retyping) every word, served as our sounding board and honest critic.

The task of finding just the right reference materials was certainly eased by the assistance, support and interest of Eileen Cooper and Helen Jacob, children's librarians from the Winnetka and Glencoe Public Libraries, and Judy Rosenthal at the Northwestern University Library of African Studies. Many of our food recipes were lovingly tested (and tasted!) in the kitchens of Carol Front and Susie Bisgeier, to whom we add yet another thank you.

Lastly, we'd like to acknowledge the youngest members of our families who tested out the many activities — Matthew and Adam Heller, Karen Haas, and especially Nancy Cole (and her Girl Scout Troop 270, Winnetka, Illinois) and Beth Weinberger, who represent the target age group for *Children Are Children Are Children.*

INTRODUCTION

Children are children are children . . . Whether they live in ancient Esfahān or modern Brasília, there are many common threads running through their childhood years. Children everywhere enjoy jacks and jump rope; hopscotch and hide and seek; ice cream, candy and birthday candles. Games like "scissors, paper, stone" — "jan ken po," "les ciseaux, le papier, la pierre" — in whatever language, have been used by children for centuries to choose up sides. Holidays are also special times for every child; whether it is a French fête, a Brazilian festa, or a Japanese matsuri, everyone feels the excitement of fireworks, singing, dancing and colorful parades.

In choosing the content for each of the six chapters of this book, the highest priority was placed on selecting subjects that would involve children, topics that would readily lend themselves to both individual and group activities and give children a sense of discovery as they explored a new and unfamiliar land.

To understand the shortage of water in Iran, a conservation project is suggested; to appreciate the skilled work of the Brazilian coffee taster, there are directions for a "tasting party"; to "get into" the meaning of the cubist art of Picasso and Braque, a group can paste up a bagful of geometric shapes . . . or, to identify with the delicate work of the Persian miniature painters, children are challenged to try out a brush with only a single hair.

This activity approach, used successfully in our first book, I Saw a Purple Cow, and our second one, A Pumpkin in a Pear Tree, is now called upon again to make a faraway country come alive Children can really "get to know" the people of another country by actually sampling their favorite games, best-loved foods, traditional crafts and special holiday celebrations and customs. Through this kind of involvement, children will begin to develop a kinship with and appreciation for children of other cultures.

The reader, or more properly, the user of this book, will not only get a picture of the unifying similarities among the six countries but, just as important, a sense of what is unique and unusual about each one. On the one hand, this might be a significant contribution by a particular country to the greater world community, such as the space discoveries and ballet of the Soviet Union, the early roots of jazz in Nigeria, and the food, perfume and fashion trends introduced to the world by the French. On the other hand, the uniqueness might simply be a local custom, holiday or feature found only in a particular region — the children's railroad in Kiev, the symbolic "S's" of the Iranian No-Ruz celebration and the brightly colored "mammy wagons" bumping around the Nigerian countryside.

In deciding which countries to choose, we looked for a geographical balance, ethnic and cultural diversity, and a blend of ancient and modern. Our six choices are not meant to be "typical of" or "to represent" or "reflect" . . . There is really no one country which could possibly typify all of Asia or Europe or Africa or North or South America. By including just six countries (rather than our original plan for sixteen!) we have been able to go into greater depth and we hope to avoid the superficial stereotyping that is often a danger in a "Children around the World" book. We were eager to get past the piñata and the wooden shoes, as well as out-of-date encyclopedic details, in favor of showing the contemporary life-styles in our particular countries.

In presenting authentic games, music, crafts, foods and customs, we have stayed as close to the original as possible. For example, the actual technique for tying the Persian knot is illustrated and exact symbols and motifs for Persian rugs are shown; the traditional procedures for the Japanese tea ceremony and the correct form for *haiku* poetry are spelled out; authentic West African drumbeats, French puppet shows and techniques for making perfumes are described in detail. Where actual ingredients or materials cannot easily be found, today's materials and methods are substituted: for example, papier-mâché for the Nigerian calabash gourd; a six-pack holder for the *furin* or Japanese mobile; stones or marbles for the knucklebones used in the Iranian game of *ashukh;* spray can lids or plastic containers of various sizes to make the *matryoshka* or Russian stacking dolls. And in anticipation of tomorrow's needs, we have included the metric equivalents for each ingredient used in the recipes.

Every section of *Children Are . . .* is meant to stimulate creativity and active play. Instead of describing a real Soviet newspaper in depth, we suggest that the readers learn both the process (and the current events of the country) by writing their own. The same is true of a French "historical fashion show," a Japanese Noh play, and a Brazilian "School of Samba." Children are even encouraged to let their imaginations carry them one step farther . . . to planning a city of the twenty-first century!

Although each chapter of *Children Are Children* contains characteristic activities of that particular country, there are also projects of a more general nature that are adaptable to the study of any country. A globe symbol is provided in the Contents to aid the reader in quickly spotting these interchangeable activities. For instance, the travelogue found in the Brazilian chapter could easily be adapted to highlight the geography and major points of interest of *any* foreign country; the same is true of the bustling bazaars (markets) of Tehrān or Kano, which provide an excellent vehicle for demonstrating foods, crafts or fashions. The globe symbol will also indicate the various craft techniques, such as papier-mâché, montage, bakers clay, dioramas, and book and puppet-making, that can be used in the activity approach to exploring other cultures.

A language page with simple phrases, and a guide to pronouncing the foreign words, can be found at the end of every chapter. Perhaps even more important than the mechanics of pronunciation is the common bond that grows as children learn to converse, using the same "everyday expressions" as their counterparts in the six countries.

This book is for teachers . . . or scout leaders or librarians or parents . . . or anyone who wants to broaden children's international understanding. The subjects included are small in proportion to those left out. The books and articles we read on the subjects of French art, fashion or cooking alone would fill a suitcase!

Children Are . . . is not meant to be a textbook in the strictest sense, but rather a guide to making the best use of textbooks and other resource materials. The authors have preselected information for the readers and designed activities to expand a child's knowledge by offering "firsthand" experiences. This deliberate screening process is meant to cut corners and save time for the teacher or group leader, and to offer "roadmarkers" to use in taking children through an overseas adventure. We hope you will then supplement these ideas with maps, picture and geography books, travel brochures, language guides, magazines and newspapers, films, or even (when possible) person-to-person contact with foreign residents, visitors and pen pals . . . all of which will enrich and deepen children's understanding of children.

CONTENTS

⊕ Activities easily adapted to other countries.

BRAZIL

Official Name: Federative Republic of Brazil

AREA	3,286,487 square miles (almost as large as all of Europe)
POPULA- TION	107,500,000 (1975 est.) (five times the population of California)
LANGUAGE	Portuguese is official language Italian, German and Japanese immigrants still use their native languages
RELIGION	93% Roman Catholic 5% Protestant (largest group is Lutheran)
CURRENCY	Cruzeiro = 10.6¢
PRINCIPAL EXPORTS	coffee pine wood raw cotton corn iron ore cocoa beans cane sugar
CLIMATE	Tropical around the Amazon, semi-arid in Northeast

1

INTRODUCTION

Brazil, the largest country in South America and the fifth largest in the world (only the Soviet Union, China, Canada and the United States have more area), is a fascinating country, rich in fertile lands, natural resources, beauty and culture. Brazil is a land of superlatives . . . with the world's longest river, largest rain forest, tallest palm trees and biggest national park, greatest waterfalls, deepest gold mine, heaviest rainfall, and even the largest oysters, freshwater fish, frogs, alligators and snakes! It is also a land full of promise, whose unofficial motto is "The country of the future." Brasília, its exciting new capital, is the best symbol of this goal.

Since most of Brazil lies in the tropics, the weather is generally hot and humid, but its mountain areas are cool and sometimes even have frost or snow. During June, July and August, which are the winter months in South America, as much as 100 inches of rain may fall in Belém, the port city at the mouth of the Amazon River. If you are planning a trip to Brazil during *your* summer vacation, especially to Pôrto Alegre in the southern part of the country, be sure to pack a heavy coat and boots. In Brazil, the farther *south* you go (away from the equator), the cooler it gets!

Over half of this gigantic country is made up of plateaus or tablelands, ideal for growing coffee beans, Brazil's largest export. However, it is in the cities bordering the Atlantic Ocean that most of the people live. The rest of the population lives in small villages or on farms, ranches and plantations, where life has changed little over the years and the marketplace and church are still the center of daily life. There is a saying that urban Brazilians have "stepped from the oxcart to the airplane," and although even now primitive oxcarts loaded with mahogany logs can be seen moving through the mud of the jungles, the best and easiest way to travel through the country is by plane. In fact, regular com-

2

muter service leaves every twenty minutes to fly the fifty-minute trip between São Paulo and Rio de Janeiro, the two largest cities.

People of many different races and nationalities live together in harmony, making Brazil a melting pot where prejudice is very rare. More than half are members of the white race, many being descendants of the Portuguese conquerors and other Europeans (Dutch, French and later German and Italian) who settled the country in the early 1600s. The rest of the population consists of blacks who were brought to Brazil as slaves to work on the sugar and cotton plantations; Indians (the original Brazilians); Asians and people of mixed blood, called *mulattos* and *cablocos.*

Brazil is still a country where there is a great economic gap between the rich and the poor, yet there is a growing middle class of teachers, businessmen and government workers.

All Brazilians take pride in living in an independent country. September 7, 1822, is the historic date when Prince Dom Pedro of Portugal, who became Brazil's first emperor, proclaimed *"Ipirange"* (Independence) — "Brazilians, our motto will be Independence or Death!"

The Brazilian people share a love for innovations, up-to-date clothing, slang, the latest jokes, music (especially the bossa nova and the samba) and their favorite holiday, Carnival. Some of the remotest villages have movie theaters and radios, sewing machines shipped from North America, and the latest fashion magazines brought in by canoe or mule! Even more striking are the 15,000 "radio schools" in the villages where children and adults receive an education via the air waves.

Travel is important in Brazil, where many people journey about the country to visit relatives, sightsee or relax at the many resorts, museums and places of interest for which the country is famous.

CITIES

Two out of three Brazilians live in cities that have beautiful flower-filled parks, cobblestone streets, ancient Portuguese-style houses alongside modern skyscrapers, white sand beaches and picturesque harbors. Each city has a unique character of its own, from the largest, São Paulo, a bustling, industrial giant, to the tiny Ouro Prêto, "Black Gold," a reconstructed "National Monument" looking much today as it did in colonial times. If you were to take a flying trip over Brazil, you would quickly see from the air the striking diversity among the cities.

Travelogue

Pretend that you are a travel commentator giving a "bird's-eye" description of Brazil's principal cities. Since you probably can't actually take the trip (unless you're very lucky!) you'll need to do some extra preparation and research. Travel books and brochures will help give you a mental picture of each city. To enliven your presentation, be sure to include the interesting facts and anecdotes that you have unearthed. You might want to use some of the following *visual aids,* along with your narration.

- a map to pinpoint the itinerary
- postcards, photographs and mementos (perhaps displayed in a scrapbook)
- sketches of your own impressions of the trip's highlights
- a filmstrip, or slide presentation

If you don't have access to commercially made materials, you can always create your own. Draw or paste pictures on a roll of adding machine tape or shelf paper, attaching each end to a wooden dowel or cardboard tube. Then slowly turn your "filmstrip" through the opening of a large box, narrating as you go.

The Itinerary

You might begin your travelogue with one of the fastest growing cities in the world, São Paulo, whose four downtown areas are ringed with factories and filled with rushing people and automobiles (Fiats, Volkswagens and Chevrolets are manufactured there). It is estimated that by 1984 there will be twenty million people living in São Paulo! Point out the famed Butantãn Institute where miniature cement igloos house hundreds of poisonous snakes, whose serums are sent all over the world as antitoxin for snake bites; Pacaembu, the gigantic sports stadium; Ibira-Puera Park, the world's largest; and the Santos Dumont Museum, named after the pioneer aviator who invented the wristwatch because he couldn't get to his pocket watch while manning the controls of his airplane. There is even a golf course where you can hit a ball from the Tropic into the Temperate Zone, since São Paulo is the only city in the world lying in both!

Your next destination might be Rio de Janeiro, the cultural center of Brazil — an exciting city with one of the most beautiful natural settings in the world. Encircled by mountains and the sea, Rio has miles and miles of white sand beaches, sixteen in all, including the famous Copacabana and Ipanema. The sheer cliffs surrounding the city have weird shapes and names to match . . . "Corcovado," The Hunchback; "Bico de Papagaio," Parrot's Beak; "Dedo de Deus," Finger of God; and "Pão de Acúcar," Sugar Loaf, a pointed rock 1,200 feet high rising from the water's edge, which now has a cable car going up to the top. Perhaps the most spectacular sight is the eleven-story concrete statue of Christ the Redeemer standing on top of Corcovado Mountain, with outstretched arms welcoming travelers to beautiful Guanabara Bay 2,300 feet below. A special railroad was built to transport the pieces of this 1,100-ton statue up the steep mountain. To capture Rio in its most festive mood, be sure to include pictures of Carnival!

Next, try a trip up the coast to Salvador in Bahía, the first capital of Brazil and the city that best retains the African culture (through music, food and dress) brought by the black slaves over four hundred years ago. Here you will find a mixture of hundreds of churches and voodoo temples, and as many religious *festas* (festivals), one for almost every day of the year! It is a city of old-world charm with pastel-colored houses with red tiled roofs, cobblestone streets and the mystical *Mercado Modelo*, the Saturday Market where gypsies read palms and medicine men sell incense and herbs. Perhaps you can sketch the houses perched precariously on the sides of steep, zigzagging roads and the tall elevator that slides up and down between the two levels of the city, connecting the mountaintop homes with the picturesque Bay of Saints.

There are many other cities that you might include, if time permits, such as Manaus in the heart of the Amazon jungle, with its famous opera house built by the wealthy European rubber barons; Belém, the port city at the mouth of the Amazon, known for its Goeldi Museum of Indian pottery and the nearby resort island of Marajó (which is almost as large as all of France); Santos, the leading coffee port, Recife, the "Venice of Brazil," and, of course, Brasília, the remarkable new capital city.

Brasília

Brasília, the ultramodern capital of Brazil, is a completely planned city built on a remote, undeveloped plateau in the center of the country. In 1957 the site was only barren land, with red earth and a few small trees, yet just three years later when the city was dedicated (although it was far from finished) it was transformed by parks, man-made lakes and tall concrete and glass skyscrapers.

The government even held a contest to choose the plan for the proposed new capital, which would soon replace the overcrowded Rio. The winning design, by architects Oscar Niemeyer and Lúcio Costa, looks something like an airplane with its wings swept back. The "fuselage" section contains the downtown area with its Plaza of the Three Powers (the three branches of the government), the president's palace, a large shopping center, hospitals, hotels, a golf course, a gigantic sports arena, a university and two airports, one large enough to land supersonic jets. There is also a most unusual cathedral built primarily underground, which has a giant crown made of curved stained-glass panels reaching to the sky. The residential, or "wing," areas of the plane are composed of *supraquadras* (super blocks) that contain large apartment buildings, schools, stores and churches. Children can walk, fly kites or ride bicycles along the safe walkways built over and under the busy streets. Greenery is everywhere, even in the parking lots, which are surrounded by jacaranda and cassia trees.

Plan a City

It is no wonder that Brazilians proudly call their new capital "the city of the twentieth century." How would *you* go about drawing up a plan for a city of the twenty-first century? If you were faced with the same situation as the Brazilians . . . 9,000 square miles in the wilderness with no roads, electricity or water, where would you start? What facilities would you need? What design would you choose?

After careful research you will be ready to draw up a blueprint and set a timetable for how long it would take to build your city. You might want to look at blueprints of your own town or school . . . or invite a city planner or architect to talk to your class.

PIONEIRO

Can you imagine what it would be like to be a *pioneiro* of Brasília, a member of one of the original families living in the first fifteen houses of the new city? They saw incredible changes take place, including an entire *supraquadra* built in just one month. A recent Brazilian visitor to the United States, whose father worked there during the early construction days of 1959, remembers playing as a child in the red mud that was everywhere and crossing a tiny stream over a rickety bridge. Today that stream is the beautiful man-made Lake Paranoa, the site of the president's elegant Alvorado Palace, "Palace of the Dawn," which is reflected in the lake's blue waters.

AMAZON RIVER

The Amazon River Basin, a jungle area covering almost half of Brazil, has been called the largest and richest "natural treasure house left on earth." Rivaling the Nile in length, the Amazon River travels 3,900 miles, beginning at the Andes Mountains of Peru and continuing at a rather slow pace until it empties into the Atlantic Ocean with a rush the Brazilians call *pororoca,* which can be heard for miles!

Pretend you are an explorer, like the early conquistadors sailing along the Amazon River searching for new lands and gold. You would see many of the *same* incredible sights . . . lush green plants and grasses and so many varieties of trees that they have never been counted — palms, brazilnuts, and enormous rubber trees (some one hundred feet high and fifteen feet around); brilliant tropical flowers including gigantic water lilies over five feet across; exotic birds, fanged and armored fish, like the deadly *piranha;* sea cows (aquatic mammals), giant tree frogs, jaguars, puma lions, great horned owls, armadillos, and even enormous bats with ghostly white faces like bulldogs. If you look quickly, you might spot huge boa snakes, "fer-de-lance" rattlesnakes, or the fearsome bushmaster, the largest poisonous snake on earth. There is even a place in the river where a thick plant forms a "natural bridge" allowing a man to walk on water!

As you glide along, an eerie feeling might come over you due to the odd mixture of screeching insects, birds and animals, followed suddenly by an unexpected moment of silence. If you were hungry, you would only have to reach out to pick a small bunch of bananas hanging from a tree near the water's edge!

JUNGLE MONTAGE

Capture the mood of the jungle! Vibrant colors of tissue paper (greens, blues, reds, pinks, oranges and yellows) will imitate the intense hues of the tropics. Make a large mural with construction paper or cardboard. For the background, overlap several layers of torn tissue scraps, using white glue diluted with water. For texture, add natural materials — bark, ferns, dried weeds, and so on.

Draw or paint some pictures of the exotic river wildlife you have observed during your journey down the Amazon. You could glue bright feathers on your parrots and toucans and decorative fabric swatches on your flower petals and butterfly wings. Use shiny foil for the rare golden orchids, and dark velvet or felt for the animal fur. Perhaps you could have a coatimundi (half raccoon, half monkey) swinging from a tree branch, a capybara (100-pound relative of the mouse) splashing near the riverbank, and a snake or crocodile sunning on a log or rock!

Rain Forest

As you travel the Amazon, your trip would take you through the largest rain forest in the world (an area covering seventy-five million acres) where rain falls almost every day and sudden thunderstorms that bring a twenty-degree drop in temperature begin and end within a matter of minutes.

TERRARIUM

Create your own miniature rain forest using an aquarium, fishbowl or wide-mouthed glass jar. Cover the bottom with small stones, sand or charcoal to absorb the water; then add a thick layer of potting soil or dirt. Gently poke in small plants, ferns and mosses, such as English baby tears, piela, silverplants, fluffy-ruffle or small maidenhair ferns. Miniature flowers, birds and butterflies, made of tissue or crepe paper and taped onto toothpicks, will add a touch of color. If your terrarium is large enough, fashion long-legged cranes, egrets, herons and flamingos from clay or papier-mâché and decorate with bright paint and bits of feathers. Complete your scene with a bamboo hut standing on stilts (made of toothpicks) and water lilies floating on a small pond (a jar lid or bottle cap filled with water).

When caring for your terrarium, water your plants only when necessary. You may leave the top open, or cover it with a piece of plastic wrap or glass, removing the covering every so often if too much moisture accumulates. Pinching back the plants when they have grown too tall will make them fuller and more beautiful.

Butterflies

The Amazon region is also known for its beautiful butterflies, especially the *Catonephilia Numilia,* whose black wings have large spots of orange and smaller ones of electric blue. Collecting and preserving butterflies is a fine hobby, which you or your friends might like to try.

CATCH YOUR OWN BUTTERFLIES

Construct a net by bending a wire coat hanger into a circle and sewing or stapling cheesecloth around the rim. Wire on a cardboard or wooden handle. After you have caught a number of butterflies, you might want to mount them in a box lid, lined with cotton or Styrofoam and covered with glass or plastic, and then seal around the edges with cloth tape. You could also preserve your butterflies between two pieces of heavy plastic or glass framed or taped together to make coasters, trays, pictures, and decorative hangings like the ones you can find in the marketplaces in Rio.

INDIANS

There are still many primitive tribes of Indians, some warlike, living in the remote Brazilian jungles far from civilization. The Waurá, a small peaceful tribe numbering less than one hundred, live deep in the Xingu National Forest, an area being preserved by the government as an example of Indian life before the coming of the white man. The Waurá women are especially known for their method of making pottery — a secret so well kept that sometimes the women were even stolen away by the other tribes!

CERAMIC POTS

If you would like to make some Waurá-style pottery, just take a ball of clay and press it into a bowl shape with your thumb and fingers. The Waurá stain the insides and outside edges of their pots with a dye made of root juice and charcoal before firing them upside down over burning logs. They often decorate the smaller pots with images of forest animals. You could use a black tempera paint or glaze on your pots.

MASKS

Other things made by the Waurá Indians might also be fun for you to try . . . a feathered headdress such as the children wear, or masks for the ceremonial rain dance. One mask called *patápu* represents a male and female fish. Cut two pieces of cardboard in the shape of the fish, or make them from papier-mâché or wood. Paint with bright colors, glue them back-to-back and tie with string. To "lure" the fish downstream, the Waurá swing their *patápus* around and around on long vines for several days, causing an eerie humming to resound throughout the forest.

TOYS AND DOLLS

Having no store-bought toys, radio or TV, Indian children spend their time swimming, wrestling, fishing, taming animals for pets, riding on huge turtles and hunting for turtle eggs. Using the natural materials of the rivers and forests, they create "model airplanes" like the ones occasionally seen on nearby primitive airstrips, or construct herons, storks and egrets out of sticks covered with the mud-clay from the river bottom. You could use modeling clay or fun dough and various kinds of wood scraps to make *your* birds and airplanes.

The girls model dolls out of this same mud-clay and, after letting them dry, paint on tiny lines of color, using the same red and dark blue natural dyes as they do on their own bodies — red from the urusu seeds and bluish-black from the ganica fruits. The boy dolls are decorated to look like animals and other jungle creatures: hawks, pumas, armadillos, etc. One doll often is painted with the privileged pattern reserved for the chief's grandson — bright red polka dots on a white body. Black beeswax (or black paint) is used for hair and as a finishing touch feathers and beads are added. If you make a "baby" doll, be sure to add a small red bracelet like the one Indian babies wear. (Theirs is made of crocheted cotton stiffened with the red dye.)

BOATS

Although the airplane has now become the most convenient way to travel in Brazil, boats still play a major role. Wherever there are waterways, there are boats — from dugout canoes made from a single tree trunk to sleek racing sculls and huge modern steamships carrying precious cargo.

In Recife, the most important port on the northern coast, you will find a wide variety of seafaring vessels. Almost every foreign ship stops there on its way to Europe or South America. There are also colorful sailboats with brightly painted hulls, bringing in mangos and pineapples. *Jangadas* (fishermen's rafts) are used only in this part of Brazil where the coral reefs along the coast can be too dangerous for other types of vessels.

JANGADA

To make a *jangada,* lash together with string seven "logs" of balsa wood, twigs, popsicle sticks or small dowels. Use a twig or a lollipop stick for a mast and a scrap of bright cloth for a sail. Miniature baskets of fish, nets and fishing tackle, a gourd of water and a small lantern for fishing at night, all a part of the gear, must be tied to your raft so they won't slide into the water. Near the stern place a small bench where the *jangadeiro,* the fisherman, sits with his pants rolled up to his knees selling fish or dozing in the sun.

Floating Stores

In Manaus you will see the same kinds of rafts, but this time they are floating stores, restaurants, and even gas stations. Perhaps the most interesting boat is the floating church (which doubles as a rectory), complete with steeple; the boat captain is also the priest, who travels up and down the rivers to the various villages, performing baptisms, weddings and other religious ceremonies. You could construct a whole fleet of Brazilian vessels — miniature sail-boats, *jangadas* and floating stores.

MILK

MILK

PETRÓ

RESTAURANTE

CARNIVAL

The most exciting *festa* (festival) in all of Brazil is Carnival, which starts the Saturday before Lent and is celebrated with masquerade balls, singing, dancing and feasting in honor of the local patron saint. The preparations and enthusiasm begin months in advance. There is little sleep; regular meals are forgotten, and children save all their money for the big day. It is said that *all* of Brazil dances for three days and on the fourth day only the street cleaners are left!

Samba Schools at Rio

The most famous *festa* is the Carnival in Rio, similar to the Mardi Gras celebration in France. The streets of Rio are gaily decorated with huge clown and devil masks placed on standards or hanging from lamp posts. Floats of pirates, sailors, witch doctors, angels with flapping wings, historical characters, and even a fire goddess with a lighted torch, parade down the wide avenues.

The highlight of the *carioca* (people of Rio) festival is the eighteen-hour pageant in which twenty *escolas de samba* (schools of samba) compete in a songwriting and dance contest. The samba schools, which started as neighborhood clubs, take great pride in putting on a spectacular show, revolving around a central theme — events in history, famous people, books, movies, and so forth. Can you imagine three thousand *cariocas,* all from one club, elaborately costumed in their school colors, singing in unison and dancing with clockwork precision as they pass in front of the reviewing stand? All of this is the culmination of a year of planning and rehearsing, fund-raising, designing and sewing — a giant undertaking to gain national honor and recognition. The day after the Carnival is over, with barely a moment to rest, the hard work begins again for next year's celebration.

Your Carnival

For *your* carnival, divide into samba groups to choose themes, and to plan costumes, dance routines and songs. A typical theme might center around the natives of Bahía, dressed all in white or in the colorful *marpreta* costumes. The girls could wear full-length cotton skirts and blouses covered with crepe paper flowers and ruffles for a "rumba" look. Pile on all of the jewelry that you can find, including ropes of beads, bangle bracelets and large loop earrings. Top off your costume with a tall headdress, perhaps made of tiers of baskets filled with colorful flowers, leaves and fruit, and tied to the head turban-fashion with a gaily printed scarf. Use food trays, paper plates or berry baskets to hold the fruit and flowers. Make your oranges, apples, grapes and pineapples from baker's clay (see p. 184) or papier-mâché (p. 145), or use real or artificial fruit along with brightly colored paper flowers.

WIND STEM →
①

CHRYSANTHEMUM

CIRCLE

DAISY

①

②

GREEN TAPE FOR CALYX

ROSE

1.

2

WIRE

CARNATION →

PAPER FLOWERS

Draw and cut out basic flower shapes from tissue, construction or crepe paper, and cut the petals as indicated. Whatever flowers you create, use wire, pipe cleaners or straws covered with green crepe paper for stems, and add paper leaves. To make a contrasting center, cover a bean, bead, or piece of wadded paper with a scrap of crepe paper and twist the ends, leaving enough to attach to the petals and stems.

Boys might choose to be the *gaúcho* (cowboy) of southern Brazil with his wide Turkish-like *bombachas* (trousers) tucked into high-topped boots with silver spurs; a studded leather belt holding a knife or a gun; a bright shirt and kerchief tied around his neck, and a broad sombrero on his head. A poncho or wool blanket with a slit for the head will complete his costume. The *gaúcho* makes a colorful figure astride his horse. He plays games, tells stories, goes to festivals, plays the guitar or accordion, eats, herds cattle, hunts, and even hears Sunday Mass . . . *all* while riding a horse. In fact, he can do almost everything on horseback except the "Chimarrita," the rhythmic folk dance where the dancers swirl and stomp and the spectators clap and sing to the staccato beat of the music.

Songwriting

Just as costumes play a significant part in the holiday festivities, so does the Carnival music. Many songs, popular all over Brazil, had their origin in the Carnival songwriting contest, with the best ones published in the newspapers. Have you ever tried to write a song? You might begin by adapting your own words to a familiar tune and varying it a little by using the samba beat, the national rhythm of Brazil.

MUSIC

Brazil is often thought of as a land of music. Everywhere you travel you will hear singing . . . the robins and wild canaries of the Amazon, the street vendors of Bahía singing out their wares, the *sambandos* at the Rio Carnival, and the world's greatest performers at the famous São Paulo Music Hall.

Brazil is also known as a land of rhythm — everyone keeps the beat, whether dancing, whistling, playing a musical instrument or just keeping time with feet or fingers. This interest in rhythm goes back to Brazil's earliest history when the native Indians used music in their religious festivals. They imitated bird sounds on bone or wooden flutes, beat drums, shook gourds filled with pebbles, or just clapped their hands. The Portuguese settlers brought in their own techniques and taught the Indians to make stringed instruments. Later, the black slaves introduced a faster, livelier rhythm. The music of Brazil is truly a blending of all three cultures and is considered by many to be the "national language" of the country.

"The Voices of the Amazon"

In the 1950s, the most popular record in Brazil (even outranking the Carnival tunes and rock and roll) was "The Voices of the Amazon," based on the actual song of the legendary "Viro Puro" bird, known as the King of Love. This tiny bird living in the jungles was first immortalized in Indian folklore and later in the music of one of Brazil's most famous composers, Heitor Villa-Lobos. But few people believed that there really was such a magical bird until a German engineer and ornithologist, Johan Dalgas Frisch, went into the jungle with an Indian guide. First he recorded the song from a great distance so he wouldn't startle the bird. Later by loudly playing his original tape he was able to attract the bird close enough to make the Vira Puro a "recording star."

BIRD CALLS

Learn to recognize the calls of various birds. Go out very early in the morning (this is their feeding time), wearing drab clothing to "camouflage" yourself. Take along a cassette recorder to capture the sounds, and a pencil and note pad to jot down your descriptions. Birds are easily frightened so it's important to move slowly and softly. Will Frisch's method of charming the birds work for you?

Modern Sounds

Today's Brazilian sounds are percussive but quiet. The bossa nova (new bass), a jazzlike sound with a Latin beat, was popularized by "The Girl from Ipanema." Besides the bossa nova, there's the well-known samba, a joyous dance of African origin with a fast, rhythmic beat, dominated by the sounds of guitar, *tamborin,* drums, *cuica* (clappers) and *agogo* (bell and striker). Other Brazilian percussion instruments include the *ganza,* a gourd-type shaker, *guido,* a scratcher producing a rasping effect, maracas and *berimbao,* which is played by tinkling a cruzeiro (coin) against its one string. Find a samba record and join the percussion section with your homemade instruments. Dance to the music, moving your feet and bending your knees with each beat!

TAMBOURINE

BEANS

MACARONI

RUBBER BAND

FOIL

MARACAS

SPORTS

By far the most important sport in Brazil is *futebol* (pronounced "fucheeball") — soccer. It is said that boys begin to practice soccer as soon as they can toddle by kicking rolled socks or tennis balls around.

All of the big cities, and even many smaller ones, have stadiums. "Maracana" in Rio de Janeiro is the largest *futebol* stadium in the world, with room for over 200,000 spectators. The sports fans take the games seriously and become so violent that a moat was built between the stands and the players to protect the athletes from the spectators.

Brazil has probably had more world championship soccer teams than any other country. When the soccer players returned to Brazil after winning the world championship in 1958, 1962, and 1970, the country declared a national holiday. Some say that next to coffee, Pelé was Brazil's most important export! Born Edson Arantes do Nascimento, but known only as Pelé, he is said to be the world's best and highest-paid soccer player. Pelé has caused a worldwide revival of interest in soccer by traveling to over forty countries, to teach and play *futebol* with thousands of children. He retired from playing soccer in the United States in 1977.

Water sports are enjoyed by everyone living along the coast; even small babies learn to swim and dive almost before they can walk. Many families spend entire days at the beach swimming, flying kites (the bird kites of Rio are particularly famous) and playing games like volleyball, *peteca,* a form of badminton, and *ferol bola,* a game that is also becoming popular on the beaches of the United States.

FEROL BOLA (A GAME FOR TWO PLAYERS)

To make your own *ferol bola* game, all you need are two wooden paddles (the actual ones are slightly larger than those used in Ping-Pong), and a hard rubber or plastic ball. (You could substitute a badminton bird or a cork with feathers.) Since Brazil is blessed with a tropical climate with warm and sunny days, many games are played outdoors. Mark off a "court" in the sand, or on a driveway or sidewalk, with a dividing line in the center. The object of the game is to hit the ball back and forth over the line without letting it fall to the ground or go out of bounds. Keep score, with the first person to reach 10 (or 20 or 100) being the winner. Sometimes the loser has to do several pushups or stand on his head! You can make up your own forfeits or penalties.

HIT THE PENNY

Put a 12- to 18-inch bamboo stick (or a broomstick) in the ground and draw a circle about five inches in diameter around it. Now place a penny, metal washer or bottlecap on top of the stick. Players stand in a circle 4 to 6 feet away and take turns trying to knock the penny off the stick by throwing another coin at it. If they knock it off and *outside* the circle, they score one point. If it drops *inside* the circle or if they miss it, they score nothing.

COFFEE

Brazil grows more coffee than any other country in the world, but coffee had to travel many miles before it found its way to the *fazendas* (plantations) of South America. From its birthplace in Ethiopia it journeyed to Arabia, accounting for its botanical name, "gahwa," or "coffee Arabica." An old Arabian legend tells about a hungry shepherd boy who, attracted by the shiny leaves and fragrant dark red berries of the coffee plant, ate a great quantity of them and discovered that they kept him awake.

The wandering "gahwa" arrived in Brazil by chance, in the pockets of a Brazilian official who, when visiting French Guiana, had been served this "strange brew" by the governor's wife and was given the seeds to take home. Thirty years later a traveler brought four seedlings to Rio de Janeiro where one of them, called the "mother plant," is still flourishing in a monastery. It is thought to be the ancestor of all the coffee groves in the Brazilian states of Rio and Minas Gerais. These areas have the ideal climate for growing coffee, with an average temperature of between 65° and 70° Fahrenheit and no damaging rainfall during the spring when the coffee trees are budding.

There is a lot more to a cup of coffee than anyone imagines — you could finish junior high *and* high school in the time it takes a coffee bean to reach your grocer's shelf! It sometimes requires up to five years of careful tending and fertilizing before the trees produce red berries ready for picking. This is done by hand, since no machine has yet been invented which can distinguish the ripe red berries from the green. Next, the red beans must be spread out to dry in the sun. Finally, they are washed and packed in burlap bags for shipment from Santos to ports all over the world where the coffee manufacturers then roast, grind and package them for sale to the grocers.

Coffee Tasting

One of the most important jobs on the coffee planta-
tion is that of the *coffee taster,* who must observe
strict "training rules" — no smoking, drinking or eating hot spicy foods. He sips from tiny "numbered"
cups of steaming black coffee placed on a turntable
and quickly spits into a bowl so that the taste is not
retained. After sampling them all with incredible
speed (as many as twenty cups in nineteen seconds),
he decides which are premium quality to be sold
worldwide.

You might find it fun to set up a coffee-tasting experiment with everyone bringing a jar of coffee
brewed beforehand at home, along with the original
package (bag or can). Start with four different
brands and then add some identical samples to see
if anyone can tell which are exactly alike! What clues
will guide you — color, aroma, taste (bitterness,
sweetness)? Try grinding some beans yourself and
make a pot of coffee. Does this coffee taste fresher
than the factory-ground kind? Compare both of
these with various types of instant coffee. Can you
tell the difference?

Now look at the cans or bags to discover where
your coffee was grown. What percentage of your
samples comes from Brazil? (Did you know that Brazil fills one out of every three cups of coffee in
America?) What other countries are represented?

Coffee "Leftovers"

With the high price of coffee these days, your parents might like some ideas for using what's left over. Store the coffee in a closed jar in the refrigerator until you are ready to use it as a substitute for water in making pumpernickel bread, honey cakes, gravy (coffee gives it a deeper color and taste) or as the base for this *gelatin dessert:*

COFFEE GELATIN DESSERT

YOU NEED:
- 1 envelope unflavored gelatin
- ¼ cup (60 ml) cold water
- 1½ cups (360 ml) strong hot coffee
- ⅓ cup (80 ml) sugar
- 1 teaspoon (5 ml) vanilla

YOU DO:
1. Soften the gelatin in the cold water.
2. Add the hot coffee and the sugar, stirring until dissolved.
3. Stir in 1 teaspoon (5 ml) vanilla.
4. Chill in individual dishes until firm. Serve with cream or spoon custard over the top. Makes 3–4 servings.

Coffee beans come in many beautiful shades of brown and can be used along with other, less expensive beans as a decorative touch to cover trays, cans, lamps or to make beads or mosaic wall hangings.

Cocoa

For those who prefer the taste of cocoa (another important Brazilian export made from the cacao bean) try a "chocolate tasting." Can you tell which drink is made with milk and which with water? Did you know that you could add powdered milk to instant cocoa to give it a richer taste? What are your favorite chocolate recipes? Bring some chocolate *doces* (sweets or candies) — like this recipe for *brigadeiro* — for everyone to test. Nothing will come in second in this contest.

BRIGADEIRO (CHOCOLATE CANDY)

YOU NEED:
- 1 14-ounce (397 gm) can sweetened condensed milk
- ¼ cup (60 ml) butter or margarine
- 4 tablespoons (60 ml) melted chocolate (semisweet or bitter)
- 1 egg
- chocolate sprinkles

YOU DO:
1. Mix all ingredients together in a pot and place over a low flame, stirring until the candy is thick enough to leave the side of the pan. (Better take turns stirring, as this is apt to take a *long* time!)
2. When cool, form into balls and roll in chocolate sprinkles.

This recipe can also be used for chocolate sauce if you cook it for a shorter time. It is delicious when spooned over ice cream and frozen, much as ice-cream bars are made.

Chocolate Beans

Chocolate beans, when freshly harvested, have no flavor at all! They must be fermented and blended, a process that is kept secret and known only to expert chocolate-makers in Brazil, Switzerland, the Netherlands and Nigeria. Like coffee, chocolate is selected by "master tasters" who must have great patience and a talent for discerning quality to succeed at their job.

BRAZILIAN FOOD

Although each region of Brazil has its own style of cooking, no matter where you are, rice, black beans (perhaps with pork or beef) and *farofa,* or manioc flour fried in oil, will be the everyday fare. Some type of fruit such as melons, oranges, pineapples or bananas, and of course coffee and tea, are usually included in every meal.

GUAVA TOAST

An early morning snack might be *guava toast* and cocoa: Preheat the oven to 375°. Spread your bread with butter, top with guava jelly and bake on a cookie sheet for 15 minutes. It's best eaten while still hot.

In the cities, the big meal of the day, the *almoco,* is served at noon when all the shops and businesses close and everyone goes home to enjoy a leisurely family lunch, and perhaps take a nap. The luncheon usually begins with a bowl of thick soup (black bean or chicken with rice) followed by the main course, which might be *feijoada,* Brazil's national dish.

FEIJOADA

YOU NEED:

2 cups (480 ml) black beans
1 teaspoon (5 ml) salt
½ teaspoon (2½ ml) black pepper
2 garlic cloves, finely minced
4 cups (960 ml or .96 L) water
2 ounces (56.7 grams) salt pork, diced
2½ cups (540 ml) canned tomatoes
1 onion, chopped
12 ounces (340 grams) linguica or chorizo sausage, sliced

1. Soak the black beans overnight, then drain.
2. Combine soaked beans with the rest of the ingredients except the sausage, bring to a gentle boil, and simmer 1½ hours, adding more water if needed.
3. Add the sausage and cook uncovered until the liquid has thickened and sausage is cooked. Serve over rice with cold sliced oranges on the side.

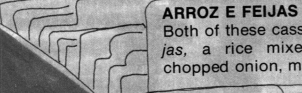

For special occasions a casserole, *empadinha de camarao* (a pastry shell filled with seafood, green olives and hearts of palm) might be included.

ARROZ E FEIJAS

Both of these casseroles are served with *arroz e feijas,* a rice mixed with chopped fresh tomato, chopped onion, minced garlic and other herbs.

Dessert may consist of ice cream, chocolate pudding, caramel custard or banana torte . . . and *doces* (sweet candies) . . . or perhaps all of them at once!

PUDIM DE LAITE CONDENSADO (CARAMEL CUSTARD)

YOU NEED:
For syrup:	½ cup (120 ml) sugar
For custard:	5 eggs
	½ cup (120 ml) sugar
	¼ teaspoon (1¼ ml) salt
	1 teaspoon (5 ml) vanilla
	3½ cups (840 ml) milk

YOU DO:

1. Cook the ½ cup sugar slowly in a skillet until it melts to a golden syrup, and pour it into a mold or Pyrex dish.
2. Beat eggs with sugar, salt and vanilla.
3. Gradually add milk and beat until smooth.
4. Pour over melted sugar syrup.
5. Set the mold or dish in a pan of *hot* water and bake at 325° F (160° C) for 60 minutes. (A knife inserted should come out clean.)

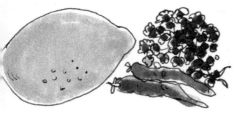

Each area of Brazil has its own distinct dishes. In the Amazon River region a specialty is *tucupi* (Indian pepperpot), which is used as a spicy cooking sauce. You might enjoy making it and discovering for yourself the old saying that "Brazilian food sings with spice!)

TUCUPI

YOU NEED:
- ½ cup (120 ml) lemon juice
- 1 or 2 "aji" peppers (or canned chili peppers), finely minced
- 2 tablespoons (30 ml) of minced onion or parsley
- ¼ cup (60 ml) peanut oil

YOU DO: Combine all ingredients and mix well.

A popular drink in the Amazon region is *Guarana*, or Indian Eye, made from the juice of a fruit similar to the coffee bean (*Guarana* is also being bottled as a soft drink and sold all over Brazil); another is *piquia*, the juice of a delicious yellow fruit in season for only one month.

CHURRASCO

The favorite food of the gaúchos is *churrasco*, a thin beefsteak grilled over an open fire, or cut into chunks and cooked on a skewer.

YOU NEED:
- ¼ cup (60 ml) lemon juice
- ¼ teaspoon (1¼ ml) salt
- ¼ teaspoon (1¼ ml) pepper
- 2 pounds (907.2 grams) beef and/or lamb cut into 1½-inch (3.7 cm) chunks

YOU DO:
1. Combine all the ingredients and marinate overnight.
2. Place meat on a skewer and grill over charcoal or under the broiler for 5 minutes on each side.
3. Serve with hot sauce.

The gaúchos often alternate linguica or chorizo sausages with the beef or lamb.

With their barbecued meat the gaúchos enjoy *polenta,* corn flour mixed with water or milk and salt and then fried. It is eaten with everything. Also popular is "eggs on horseback," two thin beefsteaks, or *bife,* pounded well and grilled or broiled, then served with a fried egg on top of each.

The Bahía area boasts of African dishes such as *vatapá,* a strong and tasty thick soup made of chicken or fish cooked with coconut milk, *farinha* or cornmeal, and *dende* oil. Another Bahían soup, *caruru,* is much like the New Orleans gumbo, even down to the okra. If you lived in the capital of Bahía, Salvador, your family would go to the market to buy *doces,* which are sold by singing *Bahíanas* (vendors) whose stores are baskets balanced on their bright yellow turbans. The candies are wrapped in fresh, green banana leaves and have fancy names such as *Beijanhos de Moça* (Maidens' Kisses), Potions of Love, Dreams, and *Papos de Anjo* (Angel Throats).

BEIJANHOS DE MOÇA (MAIDENS' KISSES)

YOU NEED:
- 2 egg whites
- 1½ cups (120 ml) sugar
- ⅛ teaspoon (⅝ ml) salt
- 1 cup (240 ml) shredded coconut
- 1 teaspoon (5 ml) vanilla
- 6-ounce (170-gram) package of chocolate bits

YOU DO:
1. Beat the egg whites until stiff; then fold in the sugar, salt, coconut, vanilla and chocolate bits.
2. Mix well and drop by teaspoons onto a greased baking pan. Bake about 10 minutes at 325° F (160° C).

COCADAS (COCONUT CANDY)

YOU NEED:
- 1 cup (240 ml) sugar
- ¼ cup (60 ml) water
- 1 cup (240 ml) shredded coconut

YOU DO:
1. Mix the sugar and water in a saucepan and cook over medium heat, stirring constantly until the "soft-ball" (230°–240° F) stage.
2. Remove from heat and beat for half a minute.
3. Add the coconut and beat for another half minute.
4. Quickly pick up a little of the mixture with a spoon and scoop it off with another spoon onto a large plate. Allow to cool. Makes 12 *cocadas*.

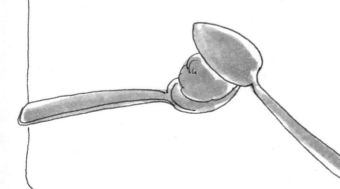

Everyone in Brazil loves bananas, from the tiny tart ones that come in bunches to the large, orange-colored variety (which sometimes grow as long as eighteen inches). Bananas can be baked with sugar or sautéed in butter and eaten as a vegetable or a dessert.

CHOCOLATE BANANAS

YOU NEED:
- 6 bananas
- 12 ounces (340 grams) chocolate bits
- ½ cup (120 ml) hot water
    - or
- ½ bag, 7 ounces (198 grams) caramels
- 1 tablespoon (15 ml) water
- wooden sticks

YOU DO:
1. Peel the bananas and cut them in half crosswise. Push a wooden stick into the cut end of each piece and put them in the freezer for an hour.
2. Melt the chocolate bits or caramels in the hot water.
3. Dip the cold bananas into the chocolate or caramel mixture to cover all surfaces. Twirl to remove excess. When the coating sets, wrap in aluminum foil and place in the freezer until ready to serve.

Pastries are enjoyed by working men and women at the *confeitarias* where they often gather for a five o'clock break. Juice bars are also popular. Here you can enjoy ices and refreshing drinks such as *abacaxi* (pineapple ice), *abacate* (avacado ice), *cuscuz* (coconut milk, sugar and tapioca flour), *refresco de coco* (coconut milk blended with sugar and ice) and even Coca-Cola.

THE BRAZILIAN LANGUAGE

Brazil is the only country in South America where the official language is Portuguese, a Romance language belonging to the Indo-European group. Written in the Roman alphabet, it derives its vocabulary primarily from Latin. Portuguese is much like Spanish, except that its pronunciation is softer and less emphatic.

Brazilian Portuguese differs somewhat from the native tongue spoken in Portugal. Brazilians have their own unique and recognizable pronunciation and have incorporated many words from the South American Indians and African slaves.

PRONUNCIATION TIPS

Vowels

a = ah (father)
u = w (win)
ei = ay (play)

e = e (bet)
ai = y (style)

i = eh (open)
ão = ow (down)
õe = oing

o = oo (too)
au = ow (how)

Consonants

Consonants are similar to those in English with these exceptions:

c = s (soft c)
h and e at the end of a word are both usually silent
lh = ly (li as in million)
m before n is silent

nh = nya
qu = k
r is slightly rolled
s at the end of a word = z

The Portuguese sound is considered nasal, and the accent is usually on the next to the last syllable unless another is indicated.

COMMON EXPRESSIONS

Hello	Aló	How are you?	Como vai?
Good morning	Bom dia	Good night	Bom noite
Please	Por favor	Thank you	Obrigado
I love you	Eu te amo	Good-bye	Adeus or até logo

What is your name?   Como se chama?
My name is _____.   Meu nome é _____.
How old are you?   Quantos ânos você?
I am _____ years old.   Eu tenho _____ anos.

Numbers

1 um	4 quatro	7 sete	10 dez
2 dois	5 cinco	8 oito	11 onze
3 três	6 seis	9 nove	12 doze

This is my _____.

mother	mãe
father	pai
brother	irmão

Minha _____.

sister	irmã
teacher	professor
friend	amigo

FRANCE

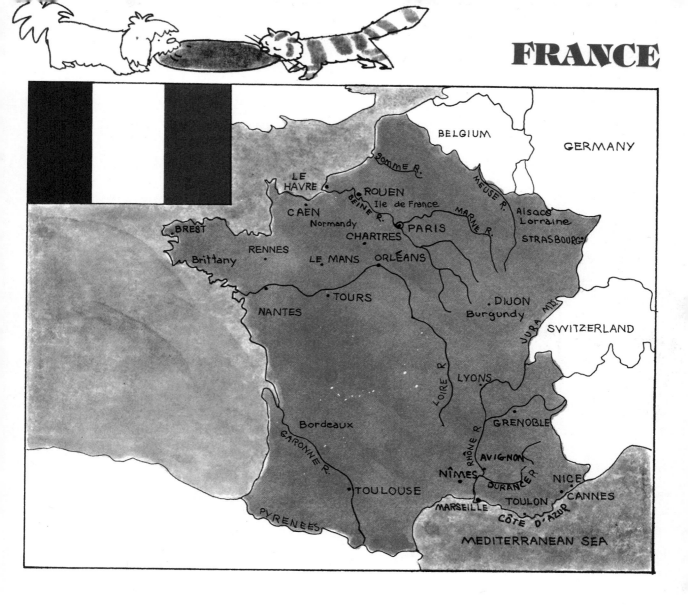

AREA	210,039 square miles (four times the size of New York state)	**RELIGION**	90% Roman Catholic 2% Protestant 1% Jewish Some Moslems and other groups
POPULA-TION	52,674,800 (1975 est.) (three times the population of New York state)	**CURRENCY**	Franc = 21.32¢ 4.69 francs = $1.00
LANGUAGE	French is official language Other: Breton in Brittany German in Alsace-Lorraine Flemish in Northeast France Spanish, Catalan and Basque in Southwest France Italian in Southeast and Corsica	**PRINCIPAL EXPORTS**	machinery steel chemicals grain textiles aircraft automobiles wine
		CLIMATE	Varied, related to area and distance from the Atlantic Ocean and Mediterranean Sea; changes sharply with the seasons, especially in the Alps

INTRODUCTION

France, often called the "gateway to Europe," is rich in history and art, and has long been a center for freedom of thought and democracy. A country slightly smaller than Texas, its snowcapped Alps provide a skiers' paradise, its Côte d'Azur (Blue Coast or Riviera), a sunny vacation spot, while its many rivers and ideal climate assure farmers fertile lands to raise wheat, vegetables and grapes for wine as well as flowers to be made into elegant French perfumes.

Paris, the French capital, is called the "City of Light," with giant floodlights illuminating the magnificent public buildings and monuments — the Eiffel Tower (*Tour Eiffel*), a well-known symbol of Paris; Notre-Dame and Sacré-Coeur cathedrals; the Louvre museum of art (included in its famous collection are the Mona Lisa, the Winged Victory of Samothrace and the Venus de Milo); the Hôtel des Invalides (Napoleon's tomb); and Sainte-Chapelle, a little jewel of stained glass. No tourist could ever forget the monument to Napoleon's victories, the Arc de Triomphe de l'Etoile, from which a dozen broad avenues radiate in all directions. Best known of these is the Champs-Elysées, a grand boulevard flanked by fashionable boutiques and sidewalk cafes.

A new and unique landmark opened in 1977 is the Beaubourg Museum (the Georges Pompidou National Center for Art and Culture), designed by an English and an Italian architect, winners of a contest in which 681 plans were submitted. Described by some as a monstrosity, this futuristic building has stirred up great controversy in the art world. It has been nicknamed the "oil refinery," the "art hangar" and *"laidbourg"* (uglyville) because of its outer steel scaffolding and exposed pipes and ducts of red, yellow, blue and green. A "building turned inside out," its most striking features in addition to the colorful pipes are the caterpillarlike glass-enclosed escalator on the outside and its outstanding collections of art and music.

Outside Paris, the sumptuous Palace of Versailles built by Louis XIV and the numerous chateaux of the Loire Valley reflect the wealth of the French royalty and nobility of a past era. Rouen, Amiens, Chartres and Reims are cities made famous by their medieval cathedrals. The Gothic style of architecture in which tall spires reached toward heaven was perfected by the French. The result of the slow, painstaking efforts of hundreds of workers, it was an engineering feat that is difficult to duplicate even with the advanced technology of the twentieth century.

Joie de vivre, a term often used in describing the French, is seen in their love of art, music, ballet and theater. Monet, Renoir and Degas were among the "Impressionist" painters who created a revolutionary art form; Ravel and Debussy translated the mood of Impressionism into music, and Bizet's *Carmen* is one of the world's great operas. The seventeenth-century dramatist Molière caused people to laugh at themselves through his genius for comedy, while today Marcel Marceau has perfected the art of pantomime. Each year the International Film Festival of Cannes attracts cinema lovers from all parts of the world. *Haute cuisine* and *haute couture* have become famous terms to describe outstanding food and fashion.

France looks back with pride on a rich, two-thousand-year heritage highlighted by important historical figures: Charlemagne (Charles the Great), who became the first Holy Roman Emperor in the ninth century; Saint Joan of Arc, a young peasant girl who rallied the French armies in 1429 to save the city of Orléans, only to be burned at the stake two years later; Napoleon Bonaparte, who conquered many lands for France and said, "When I see an empty throne I feel the urge to sit on it"; and, more recently, Charles de Gaulle, one of the more prominent presidents of the modern French Republic. Of course, no description of France would be complete without recognizing the life-saving contributions made by Madame Marie Curie through her work with radiation, and Louis Pasteur, the famous chemist, who discovered that bacteria cause many diseases. He found a way to kill these one-celled microbes by rapid heating and then quick chilling — a process that we now know as *pasteurization.*

HOLIDAYS AND FESTIVALS

The French people's love of traditions and customs is seen in their holiday celebrations, some historical and others religious in nature.

Bastille Day

La fête nationale, Bastille Day, the French national holiday, is celebrated on July 14. It marks the capture of the royal prison, or Bastille, in 1789 by angry French citizens, and the beginning of the French Revolution, which brought an end to the monarchy. The people's motto, "Liberté, Egalité et Fraternité," was inspired by the writings of Rousseau and Voltaire, and also by the liberal general, Marquis de Lafayette, who fought with Washington during the American Revolution. It is interesting that after the Bastille was destroyed, the key to the fortress was sent by General Lafayette as a gift to President Washington. Visitors may still see the key today in Washington's home in Mount Vernon. You might discuss the meaning of the important words of the French motto and find parallels in the American Bill of Rights.

Mardi Gras

The pre-Lenten festival of Mardi Gras, meaning "Fat Tuesday," is popular all over France. This joyous celebration signals the end of a long carnival season that began on Twelfth Night, January 6. Occurring on the last day before Lent, it is a time to make merry and eat large quantities of *beignets* (pronounced "bay-nyay"), thick pancakes to which left-over meat and other "forbidden foods" are often added — the last treat before the long meatless Lenten season. In the town of Nice, Mardi Gras is called "King Carnival Day" and is celebrated by a parade of clowns, horses and colorful floats led by the Carnival King, a large straw man. Revelers riding on the floats toss flower petals and confetti back and forth with spectators lining the streets.

Pretend you are living in Nice and put on your own Mardi Gras festival! Start your gala day with the "Battle of the Flowers" and end it with a masquerade ball, fireworks and the burning of the straw king. A special flat, sweet cake called *La Galette des Rois* (cake of the kings) is also served during this holiday season. It has a gilded paper crown on top and (traditionally) a bean — *fève* — hidden inside. Today a porcelain trinket is used instead and the child who finds the *fève* is crowned king or queen.

For your Mardi Gras party, bake a favorite cake, spread an almond paste in the middle, and for a festive touch top it with a gilded crown — and don't forget the *fève!*

April Fool's Day

Did you know that April Fool's Day, *Poissons d'Avril* (April Fish), originated in France? The holiday began in the 1600s when Pope Gregory changed the calendar, beginning the year on January 1 instead of the traditional April 1. Those who hadn't heard the news and were months behind schedule were called the "April Fools" or "April Fish." Children everywhere still play jokes and pranks on each other, and in France they like to stuff paper fish down one another's shirts. The children are also given chocolate fish as a treat. On April 1 *le journal* (the newspaper) reports silly news, while a newscaster typically makes outlandish announcements: for instance, "The French have arrived on Jupiter."

APRIL FOOLERS

Have each member of the class write and record a silly newscast, perhaps in a disguised voice. Then play back the tape, while the group tries to identify each announcer.

Another French custom is to send people on foolish "errands" such as hugging a tree or finding a red blade of grass. Use these, along with some ideas of your own, in a "Truth or Consequences" TV show. Make up some serious questions for the "emcee" to ask the contestants. If they miss, hand them a paper fish with a foolish errand written on it as their consequence.

On April Fool's Day people everywhere delight in playing harmless pranks on one another — changing the clocks, putting salt in the sugarbowl, and so on. What pranks do you play on your family and friends?

GAMES

Games, games and more games! French children enjoy playing *la marelle, cache-cache* and *billes* . . . and so do you! Can you guess what they are? (Hopscotch, hide-and-seek and marbles.) They also have their own version of cops and robbers (*gendarmes aux voleurs*), jump rope (*à la corde*) and jacks (*osselet*). *Osselet* means knucklebone. Originally French children used seven bones to play jacks, with one painted red for the "ball."

My Great-Aunt Lives in Tours

Younger children particularly enjoy the repetition of the old favorite, "My Great-Aunt Lives in Tours." Seated in a circle, they repeat the following jingle, adding to it as they go along. This will help you learn some new French vocabulary. If this song is unfamiliar, make up your own tune.

My great-aunt lives in Tours
In a house with a cherry tree
With *une petite souris* [a little mouse], "squeak, squeak."

My great-aunt lives in Tours
In a house with a cherry tree
With *une petite souris,* "squeak, squeak,"
With *un grand chien* [a big dog], "woof, woof."

In the next verse, children might add *une tachetée vache* (a spotted cow), "moo, moo"; *un chat de gouttière* (an alley cat), "meow, meow," etc. Once you have mastered the animals' names, try singing the whole verse in French:

Ma belle tante habite Tours
Dans une maison avec un arbre de cerise.

41

Prince of Paris

Learning to count is also easy when practiced in the context of the game "Prince of Paris."

Players sit in a circle with each one assigned a number. The leader says, "The Prince of Paris has lost his hat. Did you find it, Number———, sir?" (Leader calls a number, e.g., *cinq.*) Then the player whose number is called quickly jumps up and with arms folded across his chest responds, "What, sir, I, sir?"

Leader: "Yes, sir, you, sir."
Cinq: "Not I, sir."
Leader: "Who then, sir?"
Cinq: Number———, sir" (e.g., *trois*).

The game continues with number *trois* quickly jumping up and speaking *before* the leader has had a chance to say, "The Prince of Paris . . ." If she fails to do so, or if she does not say "sir" at the proper times, she has to change places with the leader. In this game it's a penalty to be the leader!

Charlemagne

Do you know the delightful *chanson* (song) about Charlemagne—Charles the Great? Charlemagne was the first to make school compulsory for all French children. At vacation time the children, tired of the strict discipline, sing this song to make fun of Charlemagne's revolutionary ideas.

Qui en a cette idée folle (Who had the crazy idea)
Un jour d'inventer l'école? (One day of inventing school?)
C'est ce sacré Charlemagne (It is the blessed Charlemagne)
Sacré Charlemagne (Blessed Charlemagne).

Marrons (Chestnuts)

A favorite vacation-time activity in France is marron-carving. Children gather fresh chestnuts in the many wooded areas throughout the country. They then remove the hard outer shell and carve the soft inside nut.

Try creating animals and people from chestnuts. Use toothpicks for the arms and legs, or for a variation string the chestnuts together to make interesting jewelry.

PUPPET SHOWS

The children of France enjoy street fairs that feature trained dog acts, gypsy fortune tellers and gingerbread stands selling cookie animals with names iced on top. They also love to go on outings to the park (and munch cotton candy, which they call *barbe à papa,* or papa's beard) while watching their two favorite puppet characters, Polichinelle or Guignol.

Polichinelle

Can you picture a man carrying a large folding screen under one arm and a bag of wooden puppets under the other? After surveying his surroundings, he opens his screen to make a stage, sets up his puppets and *voilà!*—an "instant theater." Become a puppeteer yourself! Choose a "front man" or helper to accompany you; he can drum up a crowd, collect the money and even talk back to Polichinelle. The helper also tries to "size up" the audience so the puppeteer can tailor his performance to each group.

When you are presenting your puppet show, think of ways to involve your audience in the actual performance. Perhaps, like Polichinelle, you can poke fun at your viewers, or even argue with them in jest. Example: "Jean, why don't your socks match?"

Polichinelle, known as Punch in England, Petroushka in Russia and Hanswurst in Germany, is a person who always sides with the "underdog" against people in authority. He is always grumbling and poking fun at *le gendarme* (the policeman), *le bourreau* (the hangman), *le diable* (the devil) and, of course, the judges and even his own wife, "la Mere Gigogne." He has reason to complain about her, since she brought him a dowry of a sack of gold and 177 children!

Guignol

In contrast to Polichinelle with his humped back, large stomach and tricornered hat, "Guignol," another popular puppet, is a much jollier character, with a little pigtail that bobs up and down at the back of his neck. He is young and good-hearted, uneducated but clever. His show is a fast and happy one and the children who come to see him know him well and delight in answering his familiar questions almost in unison.

The character Guignol occurred almost by accident. A puppeteer once heard someone in the audience exclaim, *"C'est guignolant!"* (which means "It's a scream!") and promptly put these words in the mouth of one of his characters. Everyone roared with laughter and the puppet, Guignol, was born. He became so popular that today all French glove puppets are known as "Guignols." For your Guignol, put your hand into a glove and "let your fingers do the talking."

MAKING PUPPETS

Whatever characters you choose to make, remember that they can be fashioned quite easily — just put your hand into a sock or paper bag with painted or sewn-on features, *or* make a tube puppet by stuffing a sock with newspaper (for the head), inserting a long coathanger or paper towel tube, dowel or stick (for the body), and then securing it at the neck with a string or rubber band. Other simple puppets can be made by taping paper or cardboard in the shape of people or animals to the backs of popsicle sticks or cardboard tubes. Features and clothes can be painted or glued on.

For your stage, use a tall box with an opening cut in the front and scenery glued on the back. (Or for an indoor puppet show you could hang a blanket or sheet across a doorway.) In the Polichinelle shows the puppeteers sit below the stage, and the "cast" enters from the bottom.

Chinese Shadow Show
(Hombres Chinoises)

A third type of puppet show, particularly enjoyed by French royalty in the eighteenth century, was called *ombres chinoises,* because of its similarity to the Chinese shadow show. To make shadow puppets, cut out figures from cardboard and silhouette them against a white sheet by shining a light bulb or a flashlight behind the puppets to cast a shadow. You can join the parts of each character with brad fasteners and control the movable arms, legs, head, etc. with wires. Sometimes groups of these puppets present delightful improvised dance routines and plays, and *your* jointed puppets could do the same. Include in your "repertoire" of stories such French favorites as "Minou et bootes" ("Puss in Boots") or "Le petit chaperon rouge" ("Little Red Riding-hood"), as well as some of your own.

FRENCH ART

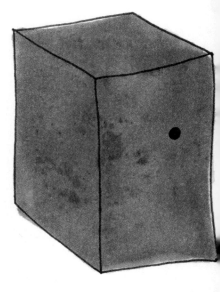

The Camera

The world's first photo was taken by a French physicist named Joseph Niépce. His camera was a great improvement over the original fifteenth-century *camera obscura,* an immense, dark box with a tiny hole in one side that let in just enough light to project an image onto the opposite wall. An artist stood inside this box, traced the outline of the image and then colored the "picture." Niépce's partner, Louis J. M. Daguerre, gave his name to an improved photographic technique known as the "daguerreotype."

Try making your own pinhole camera, or experiment with light by creating pictures made with a special light-sensitive paper. Lay an object such as a leaf or a key on top of the paper, place in the sun for ten to fifteen minutes and see what happens! This can be done indoors by using blueprint paper and a high intensity light (300–500 watts). Expose the paper to the light for five minutes or until an image appears, rinse in a pan of water and hang up to dry.

Impressionism

The invention of the camera helped bring an end to the traditional rules of French art. Once "picture-taking" was a reality, an artist was no longer needed for painting an exact reproduction of events and people. With the camera showing things as they actually appeared, the artist was now free to experiment and present his personal "vision of the world." It is not surprising that in the 1860s the revolutionary new movement called Impressionism rocked the art world . . . paintings would never again be the same!

It all began with a group of young artists who could not get into the finest French art school, "L'école des Beaux Arts," and whose paintings were continually turned down for the important exhibitions, called *salons.* The disgruntled artists, desperate to earn a living, joined together to present their own exhibition, the now famous *Salon des Refusés* (Salon of the Rejected). Their leader was Claude Monet, whose painting "Impression: Sunrise" gave the Impressionist movement its name.

For the first time in history, artists (including Renoir, Manet, Degas, Cézanne and others) ventured outdoors, away from the artificial light of their studios, to capture the effects of natural sunlight on various objects — flowers in a sunny field, light and shadows on the snow, filtered light in the woods or light reflecting off a rainy pavement. Fascinated by changes in light, Monet painted the *same* object over and over again at different times of day. These pictures showed how the sun's position in the sky altered the colors and shadows of haystacks, water lilies, cathedrals, and even the London Bridge. You might enjoy experimenting with Monet's approach.

BE AN IMPRESSIONIST

First take a stool, pad and crayons, paints or colored pencils outdoors to paint or sketch an object that interests you — flowers or a tree or a house. Then several times during the day, return to the same place to paint the same object. Record the various changes in light and color, noticing where the shadows fall. Observe carefully. Does the sky look bluer in the morning or in the late afternoon? What happens to colors just after it rains?

Impressionists tried to catch informal snatches of everyday life — street scenes, mothers and children, railroad stations. Examples of this kind of art are Toulouse-Lautrec's bright posters of cafe life, Gauguin's colorful paintings of Tahitian natives; and Degas's fleeting glimpses of race horses and ballet dancers.

You might try doing quick "impressions" of a cat stretching in the sunlight, a girl brushing out her long hair, a dog running down the street, or a baseball player sliding into home plate. Why do you think the Impressionists were called the "keyhole artists"?

YOUR OWN SALON

Set up your own *Salon des Refusés* to help you recognize and appreciate the techniques of various nineteenth-century French artists, such as those already mentioned. Divide into groups with each being responsible for researching one painter. Bring in reproductions of their work and make diagrams of the pictures as the artists might have, blocking out the main colors, indicating light and dark areas and showing the repetition of basic lines and shapes. Soon your group will begin to recognize the unique features of the artist and be able to describe these special characteristics to the class: colors, brush technique, subject matter, composition, etc. After everyone is familiar with the pictures, have a contest to see how many artists each person can match with their paintings.

A challenging activity would be to try creating a picture in the *style* of your favorite artist, using watercolors, tempera, acrylics or pastels (chalk). Pretend you are Cézanne making geometric shapes — spheres, cylinders, cones — with a palette knife; Van Gogh with his thick paints and broad brushstrokes of swirling storm clouds, gnarled tree trunks and distorted faces and colors; Daumier, drawing humorous political cartoons in somber blacks and browns; or Monet, sketching caricatures with exaggerated features as he did before taking up his palette and brush. Display all of your pictures and play a "guessing game" to see which "famous artist" created each one.

Now try experimenting with several unique styles of French art, individually or in teams:

Pointillism

Pointillism, the technique perfected by Georges Seurat, uses hundreds of dots of pure color put side by side on the canvas for the eyes to mix. For example, a green dress would be made with separate blue and yellow dots. Seurat worked slowly and painstakingly on huge canvases, completing only six major paintings in his thirty-two years! Use paint, chalk or "punch-out dots" of colored construction paper for this project . . . but like Seurat, you'll need to use patience!

Cubism

Cubism, a popular movement in Paris in the early 1900s, was strongly influenced by Cézanne. In this technique, an object, for example a bottle, was flattened out and broken down into its basic geometric shapes and shown by the artist from several views at once. For your creative activity, you could give each "team" a bag of cut-out shapes to compose a guitar player in the style of Picasso or a still life like those of Braque . . . or perhaps all the groups could try to work from the same model or object "à la cubism."

Collage

A collage or "paste-up" was a technique used by the cubists to bring texture to their art, and by Matisse in his later years when he was going blind. Collage has been described as "art made from the contents of wastebaskets" and typically included calling cards, bits of rope, newspaper scraps, and so on. If your team would like to make a collage, then fill a bag with wallpaper and cloth scraps, newsprint, magazine pictures, yarn, paper doilies, toothpicks, and straws, along with crayons, tape, glue and shelf paper for the background.

Set a time limit and after all the groups have completed their pictures, number them and display them on the wall. Each person can then try to make up appropriate "titles." Reading them aloud to the entire group is the most fun of all!

The Left Bank

The center of artist and student life in Paris is found on the *Rive Gauche* or Left Bank of the Seine River, which winds for eight miles through the city. Here many of the struggling Impressionists gathered in the sidewalk cafes to share ideas or painted together outdoors or in their tiny studios, continually learning from one another. You can set up your own Left Bank with easels, palettes, brushes, smocks and berets . . . and how could any budding "artiste" get along without his wine, French bread and cheese? When your *chefs-d'oeuvre* (masterpieces) are completed, have an art fair . . . or an auction, remembering to bid in francs!

FASHION

Who can think of fashion without the word "French" to describe it? As early as the seventeenth century, France took the lead in setting clothing trends for the whole world, coining many words which we still associate with fashion — petticoat, the bustle, crinolines, midi blouses, mini skirts, décolleté, bouffante and even the famous pompadour hairstyle.

Fashion Show

Presenting a fashion show is a creative way to learn about the history of French clothing design.

The Theme: "Three Centuries of French Fashions."

The Setting: A Parisian *salon* with a raised platform or runway surrounded by chairs.

The Couturiers: You and your friends divide into groups, with each one choosing a particular period or historical character to portray.

Props: A large box of "costumes" — long skirts, shawls, pumps, hats, wigs, jewelry, as well as large cloth scraps, ribbons, crepe paper, buttons, glue, tape, etc. (You will also need scissors, safety pins, and newspapers.)

Choose one person in each group to be the "model" while the rest serve as the "designers." Be prepared to describe your model as he or she walks down the runway.

NARRATOR: And now appearing in our show is Marie Antoinette, the most elegant lady of the eighteenth century, escorted by her husband, Louis the Sixteenth, the last French king. She is wearing a simple cotton dress, highlighted by a large straw picture hat trimmed with a flat grosgrain ribbon.

Marie Antoinette initiated the craze for "highborn" ladies to dress as peasant girls, even though she had a wardrobe filled with exquisite fashions. Each day her lady-in-waiting presented a "palette" containing cloth swatches of all her dresses so she could choose her "ensemble." (This little "vignette" could be acted out as part of the fashion show.)

Wide hoops called *paniers* were also worn in the eighteenth century. They often stretched six feet from side to side, causing the ladies to walk sideways through a doorway!

NARRATOR: Our model today is wearing several petticoats and a hoop under her embroidered dress. (If you were rich, you could afford many layers of clothing.) Her hair is piled high on her head, an elaborate process which takes so long that it is redone only occasionally. [Sometimes women even discovered birds nesting comfortably in their intricate hairdos — an ideal hiding place! Can you imagine sleeping that way?] Now to complete the eighteenth-century portion of the show, Madame du Barry is wearing a lavender satin dress over a pair of matching trousers, and a gauze turban *à la turque* (an example of the Turkish craze that swept the Paris *salons*).

Perfume was in great evidence at the court of Versailles and you might note that Madame du Barry, Madame de Pompadour and the other patronesses chose a different fragrance for each day.

NARRATOR: The designers for the nineteenth-century fashionplates have chosen apparel in the military style, popular after the French Revolution when it became unfashionable to be "fashionable." Notice the model's snappy tricolor scarf, brass buttons and matching sash over a dress looking much like a military uniform. Our next model is *très chic* in her sheer muslin gown in the "Directoire" style, with its high waistline set off by a colorful ribbon.

Here comes Empress Josephine on the arm of her husband Napoleon, who showered her with lavish silks and satins. This lovely gown of "peau de soie" is in white, her favorite color, and is the newest in her wardrobe of 676 dresses, 252 hats and head-dresses and 785 pairs of slippers!

And now for the twentieth-century couturiers featuring Christian Dior's "New Look" of 1947, a mid-calf-length dress with a plunging neckline ("décolleté") and three-quarter-length bat-wing sleeves . . . Next, another fad, a Corrèges short-skirted "nursery frock" worn with flat shoes and colored socks . . . And the popular creations of Pierre Cardin, designer of women's and men's clothing, who made a specialty of trouser-suits and to the delight of his female clients, presented them in gay colors with matching hoods. *Fini.*

PAPER DOLLS (PANDORAS)

Although fashion shows in Paris attract twentieth-century buyers from all over the world to view the season's latest creations, in the eighteenth century the vogue was to distribute Pandora dolls. These "little ambassadors of fashion" were sent throughout Europe to show the new fashions to prospective customers. You could create some paper doll Pandoras and dress them in various clothing styles. Cover the body of each doll with felt and put a small piece of felt on the back of the clothes to make them "stick." The French always sent out two dolls at a time, one dressed *en grande toilette* (full dress) and the other *en déshabille* (undressed).

PERFUME

For centuries, perfumes have been important in France and even Charlemagne used them! Perfumes bearing well-known labels like Givenchy, Lanvin, Yves Saint Laurent and Chanel, long prized by women, have more recently been produced for men.

Grasse, in the southern part of the country, is the perfume center of the world where visitors can smell the fragrance of rose petals for miles around. It takes four *tons* of rose flowers to yield just one pound of rose oil! It's no wonder that an ounce of Chanel No. 5 perfume costs over $45 and that all natural perfumes are *plus cher* (more expensive) than the synthetic ones. Good perfumes are a blend of ten to fifty ingredients, some of the most important being the fixatives that preserve the famous aromas. These are extracted from animals like the whale, beaver, civet cat and musk deer. In addition to the natural oils, fixatives and synthetics, small amounts of gums and resins like balsam and sandalwood are added to give perfume body, color and a unique fragrance. Perfume formulas, which take years to develop, are top secret, known only to *le proprieteur* (the owner) and a few trusted employees.

The word perfume comes from the Latin *per fumum* ("through smoke"), describing the burning of incense by the ancient Romans to please the gods. The oldest perfumes were made from mixtures of dried herbs and flowers, called *potpourri* ("rotten pot") by the French. They often filled small jars with roses, violets, orange blossoms, jasmine and acacia — all popular scents. Containers for potpourri can be very decorative and include lacquered boxes or old-fashioned glass candy or apothecary jars. The dried herbs and flowers of the potpourri are also put into little sacks called *sachets* and tied with ribbons.

MAKING SACHETS
Try this recipe for making your own sachet.

YOU NEED:
rose or violet petals
leaves of geranium, lemon verbena,
   herbs
wire cake rack or screen
mixing bowl
spoon
thin cotton cloth and pinking shears
powdered spices: cinnamon, cloves,
   allspice
ribbon or yarn

YOU DO:
1. Collect the flowers after the early morning dew but before the sun is high. Pick the bloom just at its peak, for if you wait too long, the essential oils will be lost.
2. Dry the leaves and petals on a wire rack (so air can circulate above and below) until they break into bits in your fingers (4 to 14 days).
3. Crumble into a ball with enough powdered spices to cover the dried mixture.
4. With pinking shears, cut the cloth into 4-inch circles and then spoon in the powdery mixture.
5. Twist the cloth and tie securely with strong thread. Add a colorful yarn or ribbon bow. The sachet can be set in a small basket or tucked away in a bureau drawer.

Perfume-Extracting

There are many different methods of extracting the "essential oils" that are found in the roots, leaves, stems, fruit, bark and seeds of herbs and flowers, as well as in the petals.

1. In Grasse, the time-consuming and costly *enfleurage* method is used: freshly picked blossoms, harvested at exactly the right moment, are rushed to the perfume factories where the petals are spread out on cold fat, which absorbs the oils and forms a *pommade.* The oils are later separated from the fat by dissolving the fat in alcohol to make perfume. Try experimenting with rose petals spread over lard in a closed container in the refrigerator. What quantity of rose petals is needed to make your own pommade?

2. Another method is *expression,* in which the peels of citrus fruit (for example, oranges) are squeezed by hydraulic presses. Can you extract oils from some citrus fruit peels with a vise or garlic press? (You might enjoy using these citrus oils in making soap.)

3. A simple perfume-making technique, and one used by the ancient Egyptians for embalming, is *distillation.* Plants (rosemary, thyme, etc.) are steamed. Vaporization and condensation take place, causing the oil to float to the top as the water sinks to the bottom.

4. *Extraction,* the method which some say produces the purest, most natural bouquet, involves using a solvent — benzene, alcohol or ether — to remove the flower oil. You probably would not want to tackle this, as the chemicals are too hazardous for children.

FOOD

French cooking is known throughout the world and there's hardly a kitchen anywhere that doesn't borrow from it. Who hasn't heard of "à la mode," "omelet," "meringue," "bouillon," "buffet," "sauté" and "soufflé"? All of these, and dozens of other familiar French words, describe foods and cooking methods that originated in France . . . from the natural meat juices, *au jus,* of the provinces to the rich sauces of the *haute cuisine* of Paris.

Pain (Bread)

The most important item on any French table is *pain* (bread), usually served at all three meals as quickly as it can get from the *boulangerie* (bakery) to the table. The *boulangerie* is a very popular spot! Every family makes a daily trip to buy a fresh warm loaf of crusty *pain.*

To make authentic French bread would take many hours of mixing, waiting for the dough to rise, punching down and kneading. However, if you have the energy, time and patience, you might enjoy the entire process. Just look in a cookbook for a French bread recipe that appeals to you. In French households there is rarely any bread left over, but if there should be, it is quickly turned into croutons, stuffing, pudding and what Americans call "French toast," which the French serve as a dessert, flavoring it with liqueur and a sprinkling of sugar or a bit of jelly.

French bread comes in many shapes, varying from village to village; it is said that the flat loaves were created to fit into a hunter's bag and the long *baguettes* were shaped for the shepherd's deep pockets . . . along with his bottle of wine. *Brioche,* a round roll, and *croissant,* a crescent-shaped roll, are popular at breakfast time. French school children eagerly look forward to their after-school *goûter* (snack) of bread and a piece of chocolate. If they save their pennies, they may be able to treat themselves to a delicious éclair, Napoleon slice or petits fours, the pastries for which the village *patisseries* are so famous. *N'est-ce pas?*

PATISSERIE

Set up your own *patisserie!* A striped awning, a card table with a checked tablecloth, a chef's hat and *voilà!* — you're in business. Don't forget a cashbox to hold your francs and centîmes (1 franc = 21¢; 100 centîmes = 1 franc). Try concocting some of these *bonbons* (sweets) for your *patisserie:*

PATISSERIE

LES PORC-EPICS SUCRÉS (SWEET PORCUPINES)

YOU NEED:
- ½ cup (120 ml) water
- 1½ cups (360 ml) sugar
- 3 eggs
- 1 teaspoon (5 ml) vanilla (optional)
- ½ teaspoon (2½ ml) salt
- 2 cups (240 ml) ground almonds
- ½ cup (120 ml) almond slivers

YOU DO:

1. *Simmer* the water and sugar in a saucepan until thickened (about 15 minutes. Do not overcook).
2. Separate the egg whites and yolks. Put the yolks in a large bowl (reserve the whites for a later meringue dish) and beat by hand.
3. Add the ground almonds, salt and vanilla to the egg yolks and mix well with a wooden spoon. Add sugar syrup.
4. Using your fingers, mold into porcupine shapes. Stick in slivers of almonds for quills. (Makes about 30 porcupines.)

PETITS FOURS

YOU NEED:

1 package yellow or white cake mix
butter cream frosting
currant jelly (optional)
food coloring (optional)

YOU DO:

1. Following the directions on the cake mix, bake in a 12 x 18 inch (30.5 x 45.7 cm) pan.
2. When cool, cut the cake into diamond shapes. Carefully lift each diamond out of the pan with a spatula and place on a rack or waxed paper.
3. Add hot water, 1 tablespoonful at a time, to the butter cream frosting until it is a good consistency to spread. Spoon it over the top and sides of each small cake. When the frosting is hard, you could drizzle melted currant jelly diluted with water over the top to give a shiny look.
4. If you wish, color some of the frosting, and using a pastry tube squeeze out flowers and other decorations on the top of each cake.

Bon appétit!

TRUFFLES (CANDY)

YOU NEED:

½ cup (120 ml) sweet butter (at room temperature)
1¼ cup (300 ml) confectioners sugar
¾ cup (180 ml) Dutch cocoa
1 egg
2 teaspoons (10 ml) rum extract or 2 teaspoons vanilla
chocolate sprinkles or coconut flakes

YOU DO:

1. Whip the butter until it is light and creamy.
2. Combine the sugar and cocoa and put through a sifter; then add half of it slowly to the butter, mixing continually.
3. Add the egg and rum extract, mix well, and then slowly add the rest of the cocoa and sugar.
4. Refrigerate the mixture for 1 hour or longer.
5. Mold into small balls and roll in chocolate sprinkles or coconut flakes. Keep refrigerated.

MERINGUE SHELLS

YOU NEED: 3 egg whites
¼ teaspoon (1¼ ml) cream of tartar
½ teaspoon (2½ ml) vanilla flavoring
1 cup (240 ml) sugar
food coloring (optional)

YOU DO:

1. In a large mixing bowl, combine egg whites with cream of tartar and beat well (medium speed on mixer).
2. Add the vanilla and sugar, and continue beating until stiff. Tint with food coloring, if you wish.
3. Using the back of a spoon, shape the meringue into eight individual shells (approximately ⅓ cup — 80 ml — meringue for each) and place on a cookie sheet covered with brown paper.
4. Bake for 1 hour at 275° F (135° C; very slow oven), then turn off the oven and leave in until cool.
5. Fill with fresh strawberries and whipping cream or ice cream and sauce.

Sundays in France are special! That's the day the bakers are the busiest, creating large, fancy *gâteaux* (cakes). The streets are filled with men balancing huge cake boxes, while the women are at home preparing the best meal of the week.

You might want to serve your cake and other pastries with ice cream, *à la mode*. Did you know that ice cream came to the United States from France? When Thomas Jefferson was ambassador to France in 1789 he tasted a new "concoction" and liked it so much that he brought this recipe home: "Take some cream, eggs and sugar and stir in a pewter bowl set over cracked ice."

Cordon Bleu

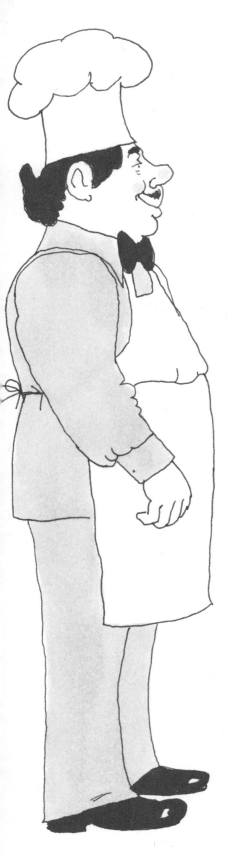

The most elaborate style of French cooking called *haute cuisine* or *la grande cuisine* is taught in the Cordon Bleu (Blue Ribbon) Cooking School of Paris, founded in 1895. Have you ever won a blue ribbon? The award itself goes back to 1578 and the "Ordre du Saint-Esprit" — an order of knights who wore a white cross on a blue ribbon. Later it came to signify special eminence in many fields, even including cooking. The first cook to receive the coveted award, it is said, was a woman who was knighted by Louis XV at the suggestion of Madame du Barry. Later, the name became associated with the famous cooking school where even today only a few of the thousands of would-be *cuisiniers* and *cuisinières* (cooks) attending its fifty sessions can win a "Cordon Bleu" diploma.

The secret of good French cooking is to make a dish taste the same *every* time you make it by using precise methods and measurements. Escoffier of the Ritz Hotels, one of the greatest French chefs, invented seven thousand recipes, relying on just five basic stocks and sauces. His motto was *"Faites simple"* — Make it simple! Basic French sauces are not difficult and make many foods more festive. You might want to experiment with one of these: *espagnole* (brown sauce made with browned butter and meat stock); *velouté* (white sauce); *béchamel* (cream sauce) — these three use a flour and butter *roux; or tomate* (tomato) and *hollandaise* (with egg yolk and butter as the base). The many names of sauces that you find in your cookbook index simply refer to a variety of ingredients added to these five basic categories.

SAUCE BÉCHAMEL

YOU NEED:
- 2 tablespoons (30 ml) flour
- 3 tablespoons (45 ml) butter
- 2 cups (480 ml) hot milk
- salt and pepper to taste
- wire whip or mixer

YOU DO:
1. Melt butter in saucepan, blend in flour and stir over moderate heat for two minutes. This is called a *roux.*
2. Remove from heat and beat in hot milk until mixture is perfectly smooth.
3. Return sauce to high heat and stir until it thickens and comes to a boil.
4. Season lightly and stir while boiling for two minutes.

Provençale Cooking

Haute cuisine owes much to the simpler cooking of the provinces (called *provençale*), even though its methods are totally different. *Provençale* cookery relies on fresh foods in their own natural juices rather than on rich sauces. Each district traditionally has its own separate culture and unique style of cooking. For example, the district of Alsace-Lorraine, with its German influence, is known for Muenster cheese and quiche Lorraine; Burgundy (Bourgogne) is famous for red Burgundy wine and mustard from Dijon, its principal city and the mustard capital of the world; Normandy for its Camembert cheese; and Brittany (Bretagne) for the thin French pancake, *la crêpe,* which was developed there.

The French love to eat their *crêpes* with jam, butter or cheese. According to an old custom, it is believed that if you flip the *crêpes* quickly in the skillet with one hand and you have a coin in your other hand, you will have good luck and money all year long!

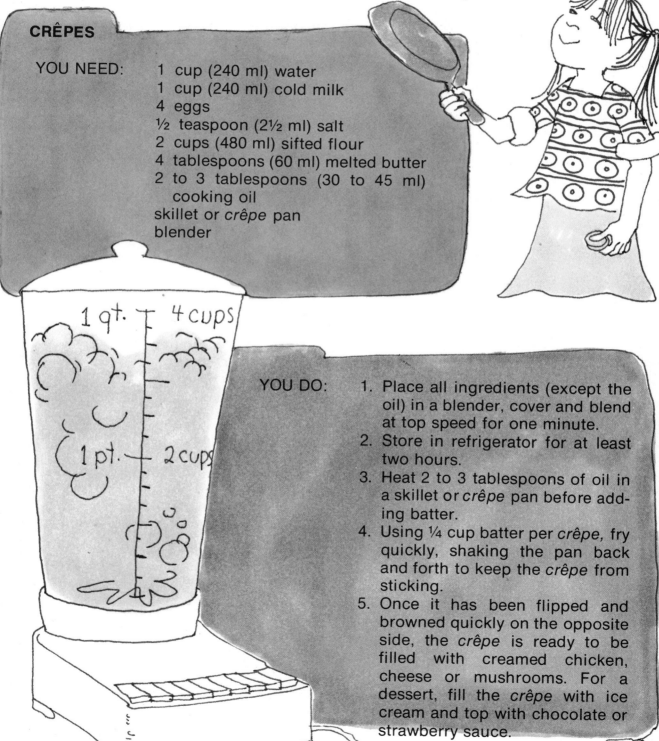

CRÊPES

YOU NEED:
- 1 cup (240 ml) water
- 1 cup (240 ml) cold milk
- 4 eggs
- ½ teaspoon (2½ ml) salt
- 2 cups (480 ml) sifted flour
- 4 tablespoons (60 ml) melted butter
- 2 to 3 tablespoons (30 to 45 ml) cooking oil
- skillet or *crêpe* pan
- blender

YOU DO:
1. Place all ingredients (except the oil) in a blender, cover and blend at top speed for one minute.
2. Store in refrigerator for at least two hours.
3. Heat 2 to 3 tablespoons of oil in a skillet or *crêpe* pan before adding batter.
4. Using ¼ cup batter per *crêpe,* fry quickly, shaking the pan back and forth to keep the *crêpe* from sticking.
5. Once it has been flipped and browned quickly on the opposite side, the *crêpe* is ready to be filled with creamed chicken, cheese or mushrooms. For a dessert, fill the *crêpe* with ice cream and top with chocolate or strawberry sauce.

QUICHE LORRAINE

Did you know that the original quiche Lorraine was made with bread dough, not pastry, and the filling was smoked bacon, cream and eggs? The addition of grated cheese is something that developed over the years as quiche Lorraine made the rounds of other countries. Perhaps you would like to try the authentic version by rolling bread dough out flat, and putting it in a tart pan before adding the fillings.

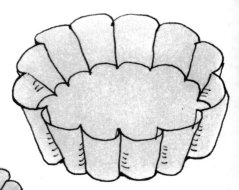

YOU NEED:
- 6 slices of crisp bacon, crumbled
- 8-inch (20.3-cm) piecrust
- 3 eggs
- 1¾ cup (420 ml) cream (half-and-half may be substituted)
- 2 to 4 tablespoons (30 to 60 ml) grated Swiss cheese
- ½ teaspoon (2½ ml) salt
- dash of pepper
- pinch of nutmeg
- 1 tablespoon (15 ml) butter

YOU DO:
1. Cover the bottom of the piecrust with bacon.
2. Beat together the eggs, cream, Swiss cheese and seasonings and pour over the bacon.
3. Dot with butter and bake at 375° (190° C) for 30 minutes.

The omelet and the soufflé are other French classics enjoyed throughout the world. The word soufflé, meaning "blown," describes a light and fluffy dessert or main dish in which egg whites are beaten to a peak, and gently folded into the basic sauce before baking. It is fun to watch the soufflé "climb" the sides of the pan; when it comes out of the oven it must be eaten at once before it falls! Look in a cookbook for omelet and soufflé recipes to try . . . the variations of possible ingredients are endless!

POMMES DE TERRE FRITES (FRENCH FRIES)

Perhaps the recipe that American children know best is *pommes de terre frites,* French fries. Actually they were not a French discovery at all, but originated in Belgium. Cut your potatoes into long, thin strips and deep-fry them in oil. Look in your cookbook for the dozens of other potato recipes that French children enjoy. Do you like yours *au gratin?*

As you can see, the French care a great deal about food! Even a family *pique-nique* in the country may include many elaborate courses, some of the world's finest *fromages* (cheeses) and, of course, wine, which, diluted with water, even the children drink.

THE FRENCH LANGUAGE

French is a Romance language derived from Latin and written in the Roman alphabet. Because the French historically had many colonies, this melodious language is spoken throughout the world (for instance, in North Africa, Canada, Vietnam). For centuries French has served as the international language of diplomats and nobility. To preserve the purity of their beautiful language, the French government recently passed a law prohibiting the media from using "franglais" (a combination of English and French words like "le weekend," "le skyscraper" and "le drugstore").

PRONUNCIATION TIPS

Vowels

a = ah (father)   é = a (mate)   è or ê = eh (met)   i = ee
o = o (cloth)   o at the end of word = o
                    (hope)   oi = wa
au/eau = o (hope)   e at the end of any word is silent (except in poetry and songs)

There is no English sound quite like the French u; to pronounce it, round your lips as if you're going to whistle and then say eee.

Consonants

c before e, i and y, and ç = s (city)   j = zh (pleasure)
c before a, o and u = k (cat)   qu = k
g before e, i and y = j (gym)   r = a guttural sound in the back of your
g before a, o and u = g (go)   throat like gargling

Final consonants are not pronounced except for c, r, f and l.

COMMON EXPRESSIONS

Hello	Allô	How are you?	Comment allez-vous?
Good morning	Bon jour	Good night	Bonne nuit
Please	S'il vous plaît	Thank you	Merci
I love you	Je t'aime	Good-bye	Au revoir

What is your name?   Comment vous appelez-vous?
My name is _____.   Je m'appelle _____.
How old are you?   Quel âge avez-vous?
I am _____ years old. J'ai _____ ans.

Numbers

1 un   4 quatre   7 sept   10 dix
2 deux   5 cinq   8 huit   11 onze
3 trois   6 six   9 neuf   12 douze

This is my _____.   *C'est _____.*

mother   ma mère   sister   ma sœur
father   mon père   teacher   mon professeur
brother   mon frère   friend   mon ami

IRAN

AREA	636,300 square miles (about 3 times the size of Texas)
POPULATION	33,000,000 (1975 est.) (Texas and California combined)
LANGUAGE	Persian or Farsi (an Indo-European language written in Arabic characters) is spoken by the majority. Non-Persian languages are Kurdish and Turkish dialects.
RELIGION	98% Moslem Minority groups include Jews, Bahais, Zoroastrians, Christian Armenians, Assyrians.
CURRENCY	Rial = 1.43¢ 70 rial = $1.00
PRINCIPAL EXPORTS	oil cotton carpets fruits
CLIMATE	Caspian, coastal area: semitropical Persian Gulf: hot and dry

INTRODUCTION

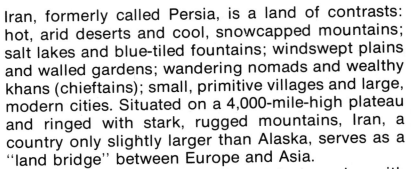

Iran, formerly called Persia, is a land of contrasts: hot, arid deserts and cool, snowcapped mountains; salt lakes and blue-tiled fountains; windswept plains and walled gardens; wandering nomads and wealthy khans (chieftains); small, primitive villages and large, modern cities. Situated on a 4,000-mile-high plateau and ringed with stark, rugged mountains, Iran, a country only slightly larger than Alaska, serves as a "land bridge" between Europe and Asia.

Persia was once the world's greatest empire, with well-built cities, magnificent palaces, a rich culture, a unique system of irrigation. The ancient capital, Persepolis, a city now being restored, stands as a reminder of the grandeur that was ancient Persia.

Today — 2,500 years later — the country of Iran is reemerging as an influential world power because of its twin bonanzas of oil and natural gas. In 1951, the oil industry became nationalized and is now the mainstay of Iran's economy. A symbol of Iran's recent progress is the "White Revolution," a series of reforms started by the first Shah (ruler) of the Pahlavi family and implemented in the 1960s by his son, the present Shah, Mohammed Reza. Through these reforms, which have greatly improved the life of the people, each farmer is given his own *hector* (parcel) of land; factory workers share in the profits; education and medical care are made available for all (in part through a unique system of military service in which educated Iranians, including women, can choose to spend their required two years of service working in hospitals or schools to improve life in remote villages); and finally, women can now vote in elections and play a larger part in the government. In fact, more than forty women are members of the *Majlis* (Parliament) and several are cabinet ministers.

The people of Iran (who call themselves *Irani*) are warm, courteous and hospitable with strong family ties, a great respect for education and a deep pride in the cultural heritage of their Indo-European and Aryan ancestors. They cherish their beautiful tiled mosques (houses of worship) and mausoleums and their traditional arts, such as the intricately hand-woven Persian rugs, delicately painted miniatures, and illuminated manuscripts of their poets, especially those of Firdowsi.

Ninety-eight percent of the Iranian people are Moslems, believers in Islam (an Arabic word meaning "submission to God"), founded by the prophet Mohammed in A.D. 622. Their creed is simple: "There is no God but Allah, and Mohammed is the messenger of Allah." There are four duties required of every Moslem: prayer, fasting during the lunar month of Ramadan, the giving of alms, and a pilgrimage to the holy city of Mecca. The sacred text of Islam is the *Koran* (reading), which contains Mohammed's teachings concerning manners, morals and religious laws. Since Friday is the day of worship in the Islamic religion, there is no school that day for the children.

Because of the harsh nature of the land and the great scarcity of water in this vast country, most of the people live either in small farm villages nestled in the mountains or in the larger cities, which are located in the western part of the country. Meshed, the holy city, known for its shrine to Imam Reza, a descendant of Mohammed, is one of the few large settlements lying east of the vast, dry desert, the Dasht-e Kavir. Among Iran's other time-honored cities are: Tabriz, the trade center of northwestern Iran and the second largest city, famous for its rugs, dried fruits and leather goods; Esfahān, a seventeenth-century "treasure house" of art with its domed mausoleums and mosques, 162 in all, including the famous *Masjid-i-shah* (Blue Mosque); Shiraz, the "city of roses and poets," with its beautiful, flower-filled parks and its main street, the *Chaha Bagh* (Four Gardens); and Abadan, which has one of the world's largest and most modern oil refineries.

Tehrān, the present capital and largest city, reflects, perhaps more than any of the other cities, the

73

fascinating mixture of old and new so characteristic of today's Iran. Here in the shadows of the towering Elburz Mountains you will find ancient mud houses standing next to beautiful modern buildings; narrow, crooked streets and wide boulevards where shiny new automobiles and motorcycles rush along at breakneck speed amid old-fashioned wagons and oxcarts. Men and women in Western clothes walk side by side with people dressed in costumes worn centuries ago. You might even glimpse teenagers whose flowing *chadors* (long veils) cover blue jeans and T-shirts emblazoned with the names of American colleges or the words Apollo II!

If you were to visit Tehrān, you would find the city laid out like a chessboard with avenues punctuated at the intersections by fountains (did you know that the game of chess was perfected in Iran hundreds of years ago?). You would want to allow plenty of time to explore the Shayad Tower, called the "gateway to Iran," with its Museum of Exhibits showing the past, present and future achievements of the country. Your favorite exhibit might be the audiovisual theater, the Cyrus Cylinder, with its 140 movie and slide projectors all going simultaneously! You would also marvel at the magnificent jeweled Peacock Throne (*Tavous*), the most expensive chair in the world, which sits in splendor in the Golestan Palace. The throne is covered with thousands of inlaid precious stones in the forms of suns, flowers, leaves and birds. The most eye-popping sight of all is the collection of crown jewels at the Bank Melli, which include a golden globe encrusted with emeralds and 50,000 other precious stones; a dazzling crown of gold and pearls; diamond and emerald necklaces; ruby rings and a small snuffbox said to be worth $5,000,000! The present Shah gave this priceless collection to the government and now he must be escorted by an armed guard to the jewel room in the bank and is asked to sign a receipt when he wants to borrow a piece of jewelry for his wife, the Empress Farah Diba. These sparkling jewels not only act as a "mortgage" for the country's debts (investments) but reflect the beauty and culture of the old Iran and the hopes and accomplishments of the new.

WATER

Perhaps the most precious thing in central Iran is water, since the mountains surrounding the giant plateau keep the rain clouds from moving over the interior. Therefore, there is little vegetation and, to make matters worse, the rivers that flow toward the center of the country dry up in the arid, desertlike soil. You can well imagine how anxiously the people in the mountain areas wait for snow, which melts in a rush in the spring, providing some of the much-needed water for drinking, bathing and watering the fields. Dasht-e Lūt, a vast desert area that archaeologists now are preserving and restoring, is said to be the driest place in the world, where even snakes and lizards cannot live! Huge reservoirs are now being constructed in this and other remote areas of Iran.

Ganats

Many centuries ago the Iranians found a way to build dams and reservoirs for storing water, and devised a complicated system of shafts and *ganats* (tunnels) for bringing the much-needed water from underground mountain springs to the villages and farmlands below. The *ganat* system ends just above each village in a stream called the *jube,* which flows through narrow stone gutters, irrigating the fields and supplying the villagers with water for their everyday household needs. Today men are still building these channels or *ganats* in much the same way as their ancestors did before them. To dig and repair a *ganat* is hard and dangerous work, with the men, called *moquannis,* often burrowing through the earth like moles. To help you understand how this ingenious system works, try this experiment:

GRAVITY EXPERIMENT

This is best done outdoors or over a sink! Attach one end of a four-foot-long rubber tube to a funnel. Stop up the other end with a glass siphon or nozzle (see illustration). Hold the nozzle end in one hand and the funnel end in the other (keeping both at the same level). Ask somebody to pour some water into the funnel until you can see it in the nozzle end. Now raise the funnel up high (about a foot). Then raise it another foot. What happens? The first time some water will spurt out of the nozzle. The second time it will spurt even higher. Why? The water flows downward due to the pull of *gravity.* This is how water is carried through *ganats* from tanks or reservoirs located on mountains or hills to cities lying at a lower level.

CONSERVATION PROJECTS

If you were an Iranian child and had to carry water in a pottery jug from a village to your home each day, how much would you need? Try estimating (then actually measure) the amount of water that your family uses for brushing teeth, drinking, washing clothes, taking a bath, cooking or doing the dishes. How many buckets of water did you need to fill your bathtub? Can you think of ways to use *less* water? Check your water meter before and after you have tried some conservation measures to see how much water your family was able to save.

Some other questions to investigate: is your water bill higher in summer or winter? How many gallons does your hot water heater hold? How much water would be wasted by leaving a faucet dripping all day? Which uses more water, a shower or a bath? Make a chart of your findings or make up a board game showing how to conserve water.

WATER CONSUMPTION

SHOWER - REGULAR - 25 GAL.
WET DOWN, SOAP,
  RINSE OFF _____ 4 GAL.

SHAVE - STOP UP SINK - 1 GAL.
    TAP RUNNING - 20 GAL.

TOILET - 5-7 GAL. PER FLUSH

TOOTHBRUSHING -
  DRINKING GLASS - 8 OZ.
  TAP RUNNING - 10 GAL.

BATH - FULL TUB - 36 GAL.

BOARD GAME

YOU NEED: cardboard
construction paper
crayons or felt pens
markers (stones, seeds, buttons, etc.)
dice or spinner

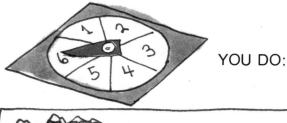

YOU DO:

1. Draw an Iranian scene on your board, laying out an underground *ganat* system. The players will move their markers through the channels from the mountain reservoir to the village *jube*.
2. Make two sets of cards: plus cards for saving water and minus cards for wasting it.
   Examples:
   Water-saving card (+): You collected rainwater to wash your hair. Move ahead to the oasis.
   Waste-water card (−): You overwatered the plants. Go back to the reservoir.
3. Each player takes a marker and uses dice or spinner to determine how many moves he can make along the *ganat.* If he lands on a plus or minus square, he draws a card from that pile and follows the directions.
4. First player to reach the village *jube* is the winner.

RAIN GAUGE

Do you know how much rain falls each year in your region? Try this experiment. During a rainy season place a bucket or other container outside to catch the rainfall. Leave it there for a whole week and then pour the water into a rain gauge.*

*You could also nail or wire your rain gauge to a fence in an open area to catch the rain directly. This is not quite as accurate as measuring the amount from a larger container because sometimes the rain falls at an angle and will not go directly into your rain gauge.

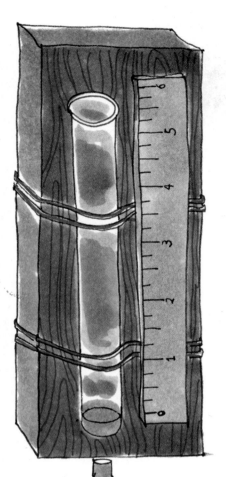

To make a rain gauge:

YOU NEED: a 1-inch diameter glass test tube (available at any hobby or hardware store) or a plastic toothbrush holder

a block of wood about 8 inches long

glue or a hammer and nails

wire or rubber bands

pencil

funnel

6-inch ruler

clay or fun dough

YOU DO:
1. Using the eraser end of a pencil, press a small amount of clay into the rounded end of the glass tube to make it level.
2. Attach the tube securely to the wood block, using wire or rubber bands.
3. Glue or nail the ruler alongside the tube as shown.
4. Carefully pour in your rainwater through a funnel to measure the amount of rainfall. Ten inches of water in the tube equals one inch of rainfall.

Isn't it surprising how long it takes to collect just one inch!

CLAY

VILLAGE AND DESERT LIFE

Farmers

Approximately 40 percent of the Iranian people are farmers in small villages, where the whole family works together to make a living. Each village is usually surrounded by high mud walls and has a colorful gate (*darvazeh*) made of bright clay tiles. Occasionally a camel is seen on the narrow dirt roads. There is a cluster of small stores, including grocery, butcher and cobbler shops, a general store, a school and a public bath. Of course, there is always a tea house (*ghavakane*) where the men gather to swap news of the day, sip tea, smoke water pipes (*ghalyan*) and listen to storytellers.

THREE-DIMENSIONAL MODEL

This picturesque Iranian scene might suggest to you a diorama or a tabletop model with buildings made of tiny boxes, clay, fun dough or folded construction paper. You might even want to make a shadow box detailing the interior of a village house. The houses with their thick mud walls and flat roofs generally have two rooms, one for the family, the other for the animals (sheep, goats, poultry, an ox and a donkey). For the roof, place sticks across the top, then a layer of damp clay and a covering of straw. You will need a sturdy rug on the floor for eating and sleeping. To keep warmer in the winter, the family will use a *korsi,* a low wooden table covered with a cloth, with a charcoal burner underneath.

"Plant" wheat, barley, rice or lentils in the fields, and several fruit trees (cherry, apricot and peach are most common) around the houses. Even the smallest villages are surrounded by poplar trees, offering a cool "oasis" from the dry countryside. Be sure to include a few basic tools needed for farming, such as wood plows, scythes and hoes.

If you add people to your scene, dress the men and boys in blue cotton shirts and long coats, black or blue baggy trousers and woolen jackets, with pleated waistbands or sashes. The women and girls would cover their heads and bodies with *chadors,* black on the streets and white or colored ones in the home.

Nomads

In contrast to the villagers who spend many generations in the same area, there are twenty-five nomadic tribes from Kurdistan, in the desert, who each spring must travel two hundred miles to find summer grasslands for their sheep and goats. The life-style of these two million nomads has changed very little in the past three thousand years; they spend most of their year planting, cultivating and harvesting their wheat before beginning the long six- or seven-week trek.

The journey is hardest on the women, who in their long, heavy skirts are laden down with bundles and often have babies strapped to their backs. The travelers must also contend with *gherbads,* round winds or miniature dust storms, which swirl about them. A scarcity of water, stifling heat and the eerie silence of the desert also make traveling difficult. Often there is only black bread, yogurt and goat cheese to eat. One-humped camels, called dromedaries, are used for carrying the heaviest bundles. (Did you know a camel can travel ten miles per hour for as long as twelve hours, take a short rest and travel twelve more miles?) There may also be horses and donkeys on the long desert trek and always *many* children.

DESERT DIORAMA

To make a three-dimensional desert scene similar to your village model, fill a large shoebox with sand. Include the nomads' tents of black goat hair and their camels, donkeys and goats. Use a mirror or aluminum foil for an oasis, the grassy spot where water bubbles up from a spring or lies in a shallow water hole. A desert oasis usually has a date tree for shade.

You can use black construction paper and small sticks to make the tents. (Occasionally you will see a white tent, which means that a schoolteacher is traveling with the group.) Include a small rug or mat inside for sleeping (it is shaken out each day and folded neatly in the corner), a goatskin bag to hold milk or yogurt, and a tall earthen jug for water. Usually there is a wooden cradle for the baby — you can make yours from cardboard. Use pipe cleaners, clothespins or fun dough to create the animals and people.

CRAFTS

Persian craftsmen are known throughout the world for their skill in painting miniatures, weaving, working with metal, leather and mosaic tiles, as well as for other crafts that have been handed down from one generation to the next.

Mosaics

The walls and domes of many of the beautiful mosques and palaces in ancient Persia, and even some of the streets, were paved with mosaics made of small glass stones and tiles. The most famous is the blue-domed Masjid-i-shah in Esfahān, making a striking contrast to the dull gray volcanic peaks surrounding the city.

The *Kashi* (enamel mosaics) are named after the skilled craftsmen of Kashan who follow an interesting procedure when creating a wall mosaic. First the design is drawn on paper and holes are punched around the borders so that a black or red powder can seep through to "sketch" the outlines on the wall. Next, the worker uses a *kashisaz* (sharp tool) to cut the small enamel tiles and then seals them together with mortar before attaching the design to the wall.

You could make a mosaic picture, pencil holder, vase or coaster by gluing small pieces of ceramic tile or "beach glass" (found from a walk along the shore of an ocean or lake) onto pieces of wood, tin cans, a cigar box or large jar lid. Let the glue dry for several hours and then paint over the entire surface with grout (available at a paint or hobby store). Quickly wipe off the stones, leaving the grout to fill in between the cracks. An easier kind of "mosaic," however, is made by tearing or cutting up small pieces of colored paper and pasting them in a decorative design onto a cardboard lid or grocery tray. A typical Persian motif would be the sun, a lotus blossom, a rosette, an animal, or the Tree of Life with its deep roots and outstretched branches.

Persian Rugs

There is an old saying in Iran, "Where my carpet is, is my home." Rugs have always played a very important role in Iranian life. Besides covering the floors of the home in a kaleidoscope of patterns, the rugs decorate the mosques and provide color for festivals, much as flags or streamers do. Prayer rugs protect the Moslem worshiper from dirt, while woven rugs close off the entrance to the nomads' tents, providing a shield from the wind and a bright contrast to the drabness of the stark desert. Silk rugs make elegant wall and table coverings and Persian carpets were once even used to pay taxes!

Although a majority of the rugs are woven in factories throughout Iran, more than a third are made by nomadic families, each known for their original designs. These include members of the Bakhtiari, Turkoman, and Qashqai tribes. Each district gives its name to a particular style for which it has become famous. The rugs, both old and new, are highly prized throughout the world, with prices varying according to the size and quality. Collectors will pay well over seven thousand dollars for a Kashan, and forty-five thousand for a Tabriz! Each year seventeen million dollars' worth of carpets is shipped to the United States alone.

Rug-making is slow, painstaking work involving tiny knots that must be tied, one at a time, by hand. Women and even children, because of their patience and small fingers, do most of the rug-making. A skilled worker can tie a knot in three or four seconds — working in shifts the rug-makers can tie ten to fourteen thousand knots a day! The knot-ends are then clipped short, giving the soft velvety appearance for which the rugs are treasured. It is not surprising that a large complicated rug made in this knot-by-knot manner can take months and even years . . . seven years, in fact, for the world's largest Persian carpet, a 35-foot square. Woven by thirty-two experts in the Esfahān School of Fine Arts, it now hangs in the Institute of Fine Arts in Tehrān.

Weavers traditionally sit on a board in front of an upright loom; in the city workshops their pattern-making is guided by the chanting of the *salim,* or foreman, while in the home the weaver follows a design drawn on squared paper that hangs from the loom. (Each square equals one knot.)

RUG DESIGNS

You may want to forgo the months and months of weaving and just enjoy *designing* a Persian rug on a sheet of graph paper with crayons, colored pencils or felt-tipped pens. The traditional patterns are bold and bright (and tend to be both floral and geometric). The decorative designs are drawn from nature, often resembling an elaborate, symmetrical garden. A typical motif is a cloud, the sky, a flower, a tree or a leaf. (The pine leaf was the forerunner of today's paisley pattern.) Usually the Persian carpet will have an important central design framed by a wide border, all executed in intricate detail with curved rather than angular lines. To the Persian eye, beauty is found in a balanced, well-organized design, and patterns are therefore repeated, often in rows, in the four corners or continuously around the entire border. (See the traditional symbols on p. 88.)

LOOMS

Some of the finest Persian carpets ever made were woven on the simplest looms. A basic wood frame is all that is needed to hold the strong vertical warp threads, with a grating to keep them tight and evenly spaced. Warp threads are separated alternately so that the weft threads are passed between them across the loom. After each row of *sehna* (knots) is tied, cut and combed down, a weft (or sometimes two) is inserted with a shuttle and then pressed down against the knots to keep them firm. The weaver continues in this manner, tying rows of individual knots and following the colors of his planned design. The more *sehna* there are in a rug, the finer the quality. There can be as many as four hundred to the square inch when using wool thread, and over seven hundred and fifty with the finest silk. The knot ends are clipped evenly to form the pile.

You can make a tiny rug by tying knots on a coarse prewoven fabric such as burlap or a needlepoint canvas, or try making a simple loom from wood or cardboard and actually weaving as you tie row upon row of Persian knots.

left handed

right handed

The knots are made by passing the yarn under one warp thread, and then around the next, leaving a pile end showing between each warp thread.

Cardboard Loom
Make notches along opposite edges of a cardboard box and wind string or yarn around the box, catching it in the notches.

Wooden-frame Loom

Nail four wooden slats together like a picture frame. Pound small nails along the top and bottom of the frame and wind string or yarn around the nails.

DYES

The dyer's art is an important part of the carpet industry, and secret recipes are passed down from generation to generation. Although chrome or synthetic dyes have now replaced the natural dyes almost exclusively in the major weaving regions, natural materials are still used today in nomadic areas. The madder root produces crimson and the indigo plant, blue — both important basic colors. Yellow is obtained from the saffron, crocus or turmeric plant, and brown from nutshells or oak bark. Nomadic rugs are known for their natural colors, the browns, beiges, grays and pearl ivories of the camels, sheep and goats they raise. You might enjoy making natural dyes and experimenting with them as paints for your designs.

Since madder root and indigo are more available in the Mideast than in the West, you could substitute other natural materials:

YOU NEED: for yellow: saffron, crocuses, daffodils or yellow onion skins

for green: young grass, broccoli, spinach, escarole, moss, rhubarb or birch leaves

for blue: blueberries

for brown: plums, coffee, tea or walnut shells

YOU DO:
1. Wash and chop up the raw material, place in a pot (enamel is best) and cover with water.
2. Boil for at least 5 minutes (longer to make colors darker).
3. Strain through a colander lined with cheesecloth or a clean rag.

The traditional carpet designs and colors reflect the Persian belief in the power of symbols. You might choose from some of these when creating your own Persian-type designs.

The Tree of Life is an ancient symbol signifying the eternity of the soul.

White means grief.

A heron represents long life.

A camel symbolizes wealth.

A dog represents protection from sickness (this is based on the story of the sacred dog who preceded Mohammed to Mecca).

Blue stands for heaven.

A cock signifies victory in battle.

A pomegranate represents abundance.

The carnation, a favorite symbol of weavers, stands for happiness.

Persian Miniatures

As masters of the miniature, Persian artists created an art form unequaled anywhere in the world. They illustrated their books with as much attention to symbols and decorative detail as the weavers gave to their carpets. During the Golden Age of Persia in the sixteenth and seventeenth centuries, skilled artisans spent many hours decorating the pages of the Koran, the holy book of the Moslem religion, and other manuscripts with pictures so tiny and delicate that it is said that a paintbrush with only a single hair was used!

The most famous artist was Behzad, who with five hundred students in his school of miniature at Tabriz brought the fantasy of Persia's beautiful poetry to life with minutely detailed pictures painted in gold, silver and other dazzling colors.

You might want to paint some miniatures, or "illuminate" a favorite poem (or one you have written yourself). First copy the poem in your best handwriting or try the art of *calligraphy* (a stylized way of writing, using India [black] ink and special penpoints). When illustrating your poem or story, be sure to follow the two-dimensional Persian style of art, in which no depth is shown. Don't include any people unless they are hidden in the design, for the ancient Islamic religion did not approve of representations of men or women.

POETRY

Poetry is so popular in Iran that it is a regular feature in the daily newspaper! Young people often gather together to listen to recitals by their favorite poets, just as American teenagers might attend a rock concert. Iranians not only enjoy contemporary poetry, but also appreciate the work of writers of past centuries, such as the popular Hafiz, whose wise sayings and proverbs are written in simple language. The "Homer of Iran" is the poet Firdowsi, whose epic poem of sixty thousand verses, *Shah Nameh* (Book of Kings), is still enjoyed and understood today, one thousand years after it was written!

Persians have traditionally expressed their history

and philosophy through verse. Perhaps the poem best known throughout the world is the twelfth-century *Rubaiyat* of Omar Khayyám, the Tentmaker, which has been translated into many languages. "Rubaiyat" means a collection of quatrains (four-line stanzas); Omar uses an *aaba* rhyming pattern in his verses, as in this famous one:

> A Book of Verses underneath the Bough
> A Jug of Wine, a Loaf of Bread — and Thou
> Beside me singing in the Wilderness —
> Ah, Wilderness were Paradise enow!

If you like to write poetry, try the four-line form of the *Rubaiyat,* choosing from some of the themes treasured by the Persians: love and friendship; beauty; the relationship between man and God; great deeds of heroes; courage; the search for greatness in ordinary, everyday happenings.

Making a Book

You may also want to collect these or other poems or stories and bind them into a book in the Persian fashion. It is said that Persian bookbindings, with their molded and tooled designs, were the most beautiful ever produced.

To make your book cover, first glue three layers of cardboard together and let dry thoroughly. Next, dampen the top layer with a sponge and press or hammer in the designs or indentations with an orange stick, spoon or objects of various shapes — bottlecaps, coins, spools, etc.

MARBLING

Marbling, a technique used for decorating endpapers in bookbinding, is an old art that can be traced back to fifteenth-century Persia. The marble effect is achieved by dipping a paper into a solution that has swirling colors "floating" on top. The ancient Persians used tragacanth (a plant gum like resin) and water mixed with ox bile to make their colors float. You can simulate this process and make some beautiful endpapers to glue into the inside covers of your poetry books.

YOU NEED:
- oil paints
- kerosene
- unflavored gelatin
- water
- comb
- paper

YOU DO:
1. Thin down oil paints with some kerosene.
2. Mix water and gelatin together (about ½ inch deep in a shallow pan).
3. Squirt a few drops of oil paint on top of the water/gelatin mixture. (Experiment with the proportion of gelatin to water and kerosene to paint; when you achieve the right balance, the paint will float on top of the water.)
4. To make the patterns, swirl a comb (with some teeth missing) across the top of the water in different directions.
5. Then carefully place a sheet of drawing paper on top of the design. Tap the paper with a popsicle stick to force out air bubbles and then lift the paper off, flipping it over quickly, and drain it on a stack of newspapers or paper toweling.

Note: For another marbleized effect, you can sprinkle powder paints (a less expensive substitute for oil paints) on an oil and water mixture (without the gelatin), or use a fingerpainting technique.

The Persians used established patterns and colors that were highly prized. Because they had the skill to duplicate their designs again and again, they were able to give them names. Can you make up appropriate names for *your* designs? Do you think that you could reproduce the same design more than once?

Now that you have made your book covers and endpapers, you are ready actually to put together a book for your illustrated poems and stories.

YOU NEED:

- 2 book covers
- 2 endpapers
- 4 to 6 pieces of paper, which when folded in half are slightly smaller than the book covers
- a piece of heavy, sticky tape 3 inches longer than the cover
- a strip of paper
- needle and sturdy thread (nylon works well)
- scissors
- glue

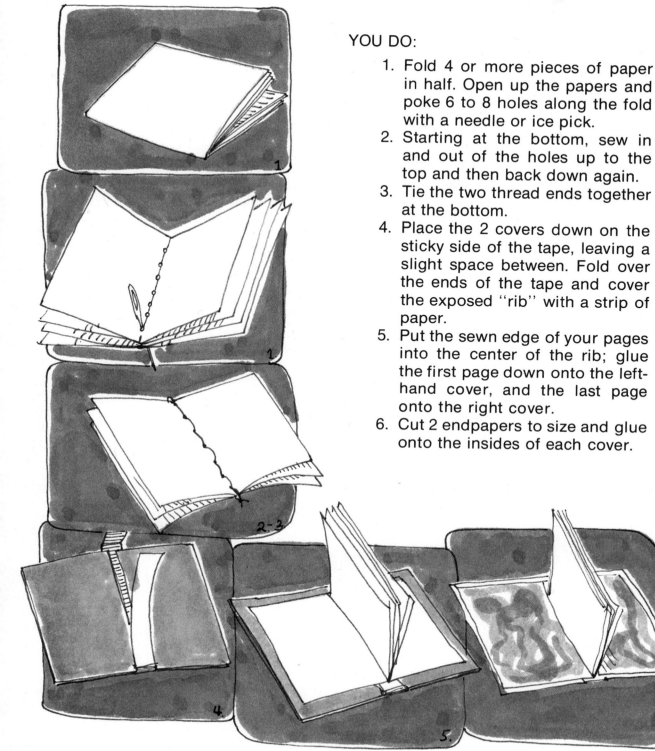

YOU DO:

1. Fold 4 or more pieces of paper in half. Open up the papers and poke 6 to 8 holes along the fold with a needle or ice pick.
2. Starting at the bottom, sew in and out of the holes up to the top and then back down again.
3. Tie the two thread ends together at the bottom.
4. Place the 2 covers down on the sticky side of the tape, leaving a slight space between. Fold over the ends of the tape and cover the exposed "rib" with a strip of paper.
5. Put the sewn edge of your pages into the center of the rib; glue the first page down onto the left-hand cover, and the last page onto the right cover.
6. Cut 2 endpapers to size and glue onto the insides of each cover.

Note: If you have already written and illustrated single pages, you can paste each one carefully onto the blank pages of the bound book.

THE CENTRAL BAZAAR

The Central Bazaar in Tehran is really a city within a city. It is the world's largest enclosed marketplace, with ten kilometers of covered streets! Once the center of *all* city life, social, political, and commercial, it is still today an opinion place where ideas are traded along with the merchandise. The six thousand stalls and shops are alive with the sights, sounds and smells of the East: thousands of voices chattering and bargaining in Farsi, the spoken language of Iran; merchants carrying heavy bundles on their backs, rushing from the loading docks to the stalls; the aroma of leather, spices and freshly baked bread filling the air. No wonder the bazaar is often called the supermarket of the Orient!

Over half of the Central Bazaar is devoted to buying and selling the world-famous hand-knotted Persian rugs. Rug sellers from Kashan, Esfahān, Tabriz, Kerman, Hamadam and other districts bring their magnificent carpets in glowing colors and traditional patterns to the huge marketplace.

Buy your
Pomegranate
juice
here →

MINI-BAZAAR
You might want to turn your classroom into a mini-Iranian bazaar complete with covered stalls. Display your "exotic wares" right on the floor or on tables draped with colorful cotton cloths. You'll want to *group* your specialties as they do in Iran — rugs, shoes, clothes, food, handicrafts, books, tinware, jewelry, household appliances, etc. Be sure to include *your* version of "jewelry" made of precious stones, copper urns, clay pottery, mosaic tiles and

leather wallets and purses. Those who choose to be food vendors would sell melons, dried fruits, *non* (bread) and *ajil,* a mixture of grains, nuts, dates and raisins. However, no young merchant could possibly afford to sell caviar, which comes from Bandar-e Pahlavi, a region bordering the Caspian Sea. Caviar is such a precious commodity in Iran that the fisheries are almost as closely guarded as the jewels in the Bank Melli!

Speaking of what is precious in Iran, be sure to include *watersellers* in your market! Your thirsty customers will also want to sample pomegranate juice, the bright red liquid used by both ancient and modern physicians as a health cure. If you happen to browse in one of the souvenir shops just outside the main entrance to the bazaar, you will probably be offered *chai* (tea) by the friendly shopkeepers whether you buy anything or not.

NO-RUZ (New Year's Day)

The favorite holiday in Iran is called *No-Ruz*, meaning "the new day." Beginning on the first day of spring, March 21, and lasting for twelve days, it has been celebrated for over 2,500 years. Preparations for the holiday begin a month ahead, with a thorough housecleaning called *kahneh takani*, as well as painting, gardening, shopping, cooking and sewing. Everything must be like new! The children especially like to help blanch almonds for the *bâglâva*, or candied treat. Since it is quite difficult to make *bâglâva*, here is another almond recipe that you can make at home or in your classroom.

BRITTLED ALMONDS

YOU NEED:
- 2 cups (480 ml) sugar
- pinch of cream of tartar
- 2 cups (480 ml) almonds, split in halves
- ½ cup (120 ml) water
- 1 teaspoon (5 ml) lemon extract

YOU DO:
1. Blanch the almonds by carefully pouring boiling water over them for sixty seconds. Drain and pinch or rub off the skins.
2. Pour water and sugar into the saucepan. Stir until dissolved, then add cream of tartar.
3. Heat on stove to 315° F (157° C) on candy thermometer, or the "hard-crack" stage.
4. Add the lemon extract.
5. Place the almonds in a buttered pan and pour the boiling syrup over them. Let cool and cut into squares.

Sabzeh (Symbol of Spring)

Two weeks before the celebration, each family plants the *sabzeh,* wheat, lentil or barley seeds. If you don't have wheat or barley, try planting some lentil, watercress, sunflower or grass seeds in a small container of soil or on a damp sponge in a saucer. Water a little each day and soon you will have sprouts.

Chahar Shanbeh Sori (Last Wednesday of the Year)

On the Wednesday before *No-Ruz,* each family lights small bonfires outdoors. Everyone jumps over the fire singing, "Take away my yellow color; I'll take your reddish hue," which means an end to winter's drabness and the beginning of summer's warmth.

Finally the great night comes! The cannons boom to announce the exact time of the "vernal equinox" (the spring date when day and night are of equal length) and the happy celebration begins. Everyone will be wearing something new and all the children will receive gifts — a toy, a coin, jewelry, a plant or a flower. On *that* night everyone feels rich!

No-Ruz Dinner

Pretend that you are an Iranian family and plan a special *No-Ruz* dinner. Perhaps you will serve your meal on a white cloth placed on the floor (no shoes are allowed). There must be at least seven foods beginning with the letter "S" (*haft sin*), symbols of the goodness of Allah: *sib* (apple), *serkeh* (vinegar), *sir* (garlic, to chase away the evil spirits), *somaq* (an often-used spice in *chelo kabob* and a symbol of good life), *samanu* (a sweet meat), and *sekeh* (a gold or silver piece, symbol of wealth), and of course the *sabzeh.* The traditional dinner also includes jujube fruit, olives, smoked fish, a sweet pudding made of wheat, as well as bread, eggs, yogurt, cheese and candy.

For the occasion you will also need to assemble

the following traditional items symbolizing the new year: lighted candles, a dish of brightly colored eggs placed on a mirror, a bowl with goldfish swimming in it, a jar of rose water and the Koran. Iranian children eagerly watch to see if the eggs will tremble. (According to an old legend they do, probably because of the booming cannons.)

Cizdah Bedar
(The Thirteenth Day)

The number thirteen is thought to be unlucky in Iran, so on that day at the close of *No-Ruz,* everyone leaves home and goes to the country. If a girl wants to get married during the coming year, she secretly goes with two or three of her friends in search of *sabzeh* long enough to braid as a symbol of good luck. For your celebration of *Cizdah-Bedar,* you might have a picnic. Bring along a basket of food and a samovar (a metal urn with a spigot used to boil water) for tea, which is the national drink, even for children. Remember that in Iran there is no picnicking on the grass, because it's so precious!

Can you imagine clowns, wrestlers, tightrope walkers and dancers performing at a picnic? This is not at all unusual at a *No-Ruz* picnic in Iran. Plan some special entertainment accompanied by horns and drums and tambourines. Bring this special family day to a close by throwing the *sabzeh* into a running stream, as the Iranians do, to symbolize the end of old quarrels, unhappiness and bad luck.

WEDDING

One of the biggest events of any Iranian girl's life is her wedding. If you would like to act out a typical Iranian wedding, you will need the following costumes and props: *red* dress and white veil for the bride, and perhaps an embroidered coat; a ring (with a large diamond, if the groom is rich); gifts from the groom's family, such as a tray, candlesticks, a lacquered chest and the Koran, handwritten and decorated in gold. You'll have to put your best artist to work on this project! If the family is poor, there might be only one gift, a silver or copper samovar.

For the ceremony, be sure the bride is sitting on the floor with the Koran on her lap, facing toward Mecca (not East — remember you're in Iran!). In front of her is a mirror with candles on each side. Not so long ago when a woman wore a protective veil, a groom actually saw his bride's face for the very first time reflected in the mirror. Other items included in every wedding are a sugar cone (a symbol of sweet married life), a green leaf floating in a dish of water, yogurt and a decorated loaf of bread, over a yard long and eighteen inches wide.

YOGURT

The wedding bread is baked in a special oven — actually an enormous room covered with thousands of tiny heated stones (*sangac*) — that can bake twenty of these huge loaves to a golden brown in only three minutes!

A very important person in the wedding is the *mullah,* or religious man, dressed in a long coat and a turban, who performs the ceremony, draws up a contract and reads from the Koran. He will ask the couple if they are willing to be man and wife.

Afterward everyone joins in a festive procession often led by a gaily decorated horse!

The actual wedding feast doesn't take place until several weeks later, and sometimes lasts for seven days. Storytellers and actors entertain the guests by chanting legends and putting on plays. And, of course, there is always much feasting and dancing.

SPORTS AND GAMES

Among the current Shah's many reforms has been a program of games to make the children strong and healthy. There are more than three hundred sports clubs in Iran and every school has its volleyball, soccer, basketball and tennis teams. Mountain climbing, archery, horseback riding and polo, which was invented in Iran, are also popular sports. Skiers can be seen whizzing down Mount Damavand, the highest mountain in the Middle East.

The children also enjoy marble games played with date pits or bottlecaps; soccer, with balls made of rolled-up rags; wrestling; and for the very wealthy, hunting — tigers, bears, panthers, jackals, foxes, sheep, gazelles and even pigs.

Alak Do Lak

Alak Do Lak is a centuries-old game especially favored by men and boys. Much like baseball, it is played with a bat and a short piece of wood for a ball. Players in the field try to catch the flying piece as it is batted into the air. The player who catches it tries to tag one of the runners before he reaches a base or home plate.

A similar game is played in which each child, in turn, tosses a wooden matchbox. If it lands on its side, the thrower becomes the minister; if on its end, he becomes the king; if the matchbox lands on its widest surface, the thrower becomes the thief who must follow the commands of the king. Can you think of some commands for the thief?

Ashukh (Knucklebones)

This is a game for four to eight players somewhat like marbles. Draw a large ring (up to 15 feet across) on the ground or in the sand. Place several sheep knucklebones, painted in bright colors, in the center of the ring. You could use small stones or marbles if you can't find any knucklebones! Each player in turn twirls a small bone between his thumb and forefinger and tries to "shoot" the other bones out of the circle, being sure his "shooter" stays *inside* the circle.

Goosh Ve Damagh (Ear and Nose)

The players sit in a circle chanting a rhyme:

A la hop, sang torop,
Peshgel box knoda biamorx hop!

One player is chosen as chief to direct the game. She lightly tweaks the ear or nose or hair of the player on her left, who then must do the same thing to his neighbor. And so on, all around the circle. After all have been tweaked, the jingle is chanted again and the new chief begins another action — perhaps a tickle or a poke. Whoever laughs or giggles or makes *any* noise is out of the game. The player who can keep the straightest face has the best chance of being the winner.

FOOD

Iranians are known for their hospitality, every guest being considered "God's gift." Visitors to even the lowliest tent of a wandering tribe will probably be invited to share in the family's food, even if it is only sweetened tea from a metal samovar, or *arak* made from fermented coconut milk. Visitors to the neighboring villages will probably be offered goat's milk, *sharbart* (a cool fruit drink), *mâst* (yogurt) and *tanook* (a wafer-thin bread). There may even be a tasty spread of walnuts and raisins crushed into a paste, or *ash,* a thick soup of vegetables and rice. Grapes, melons, figs, pomegranates and other fruits are usually plentiful on the small farms that dot the countryside. Pomegranates are used in soups, sauces, desserts, and even for a drink. Children suck the fruit through a hole in the skin, much as we do an orange. The grapes are particularly delightful and come in nearly fifty varieties, from the small, honeysweet *kishmish* to the *sahebi,* as large as a man's thumb.

Yogurt

Mâst (yogurt) is the food of rich and poor alike. It is considered a panacea, or cure-all, and a means for living a longer life. It is sometimes recommended by doctors for various ailments, including sunburn, and is even used as a facial!

Yogurt is served with meals as a soup or as a dessert, along with sugar, fresh or canned fruit, preserves or honey. In hot weather the yogurt is diluted with water and fortified with salt to make a drink called *abdug.* Iranian vendors have even been known to advertise "a jug of *abdug*" instead of the wine in Omar's famous poem!

To Make Yogurt

YOU NEED:
1. 1 quart (.946 L) milk
2. 2 tablespoons (30 ml) of commercial yogurt to use as a "starter"

YOU DO:
1. Boil the milk and let it cool slightly.
2. Dissolve the yogurt in a cup or bowl with some of the warm milk. When thoroughly dissolved, pour it into the rest of the milk and mix well.
3. Pour into glass or crockery bowls and cover with waxed paper. (If using a large crockery bowl, place a plate on top and wrap 3 or 4 dishtowels around the top and sides.) Let stand overnight (away from drafts), then store in refrigerator. The yogurt will keep for several days.

Save some of this homemade mixture as your "starter" for a new batch. If you wish a richer custard, add a pint of cream to the milk before boiling. Then wrap the yogurt in cheesecloth and hang it over the sink for 25 to 30 minutes until all of the water runs out. (It should have the consistency of cottage cheese.)

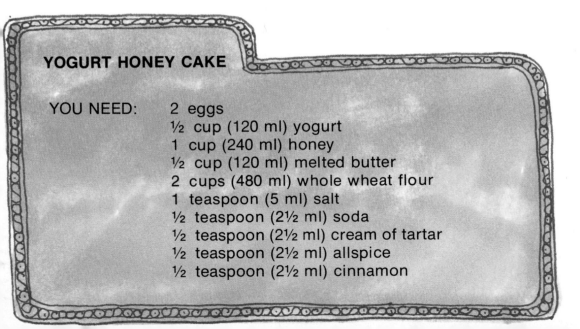

YOGURT HONEY CAKE

YOU NEED:
- 2 eggs
- ½ cup (120 ml) yogurt
- 1 cup (240 ml) honey
- ½ cup (120 ml) melted butter
- 2 cups (480 ml) whole wheat flour
- 1 teaspoon (5 ml) salt
- ½ teaspoon (2½ ml) soda
- ½ teaspoon (2½ ml) cream of tartar
- ½ teaspoon (2½ ml) allspice
- ½ teaspoon (2½ ml) cinnamon

FOR THE TOPPING:

½–¾ (120–180 ml) cup honey
chopped nuts
cinnamon

YOU DO:
1. Beat the eggs well, then mix in the yogurt, honey and butter and blend thoroughly.
2. Sift together the flour, soda and spices and add to the egg mixture, stirring until smooth.
3. Pour into a large greased pan and bake at 350° F (180° C) for 30 minutes.
4. For the topping, melt the honey, add chopped nuts and cinnamon and spread over the cake while it is still warm.

If you were to visit the household of a wealthy Iranian living in the city, he would insist that you have a cup of tea, no matter what the time of day. It would be served in small glasses with a sugar cube to hold in your mouth. Spoons and forks are now used for eating, although the old custom was to use only your fingers and a piece of folded bread. You would probably be served an omelet or a *chelo kabob,* the national dish of Iran, made from rice, marinated lamb, yogurt, a raw egg and sumac.

CHELO

Chelo is a mound of rice with melted butter in the center, surrounded by more rice garnished with saffron or diced, cooked tomato bits. It is traditionally served with charcoal-broiled lamb that has been marinated in lemon juice and grated onion for one to three days.

There are always bowls of fruit filled with "eggs of the sun" (apricots), orange or melon slices, honey, nuts and glazed fruits. *Khoreshes* (rich sauces) topped with almonds, orange peels, pistachios and dates go with everything.

ORANGE APRICOT BALLS

YOU NEED:
1 pound (453.6 grams) dried apricots
1 4-ounce (113 grams) package shredded coconut
⅓ cup (80 ml) sugar
1 orange, peeled and sectioned with white membrane removed

YOU DO:
1. Grind apricots and orange.
2. Stir in sugar and let stand until sugar is dissolved.
3. Shape into balls and roll in the coconut.

Fruit salads are also popular and are eaten with or after the main meal.

SHAH'S SALAD

This salad consists of small pieces of cooked lamb and melon balls tossed with a special yogurt dressing and served in scooped-out melon halves.

YOGURT DRESSING:

3 cups (720 ml) yogurt
a bunch of seedless grapes
1 teaspoon (5 ml) honey
1 cup (240 ml) pineapple juice
1 teaspoon (5 ml) almond extract
½ cup (120 ml) chopped walnuts

Iranians love green salads. If fresh vegetables are not available, the housewife usually has some dried vegetables stored away in her *anbâr,* or pantry.

A special treat in an Iranian home is decorative marzipan candy, which looks almost too good to eat!

MARZIPAN

YOU NEED:

1 cup (240 ml) almond paste
2 egg whites (whipped separately)
½ teaspoon (2½ ml) vanilla extract
3 to 4 cups (720 to 960 ml) confectioners sugar
food coloring

YOU DO:

1. Place the almond paste in a bowl and knead with your hands.
2. Add 1 egg white and then the other, kneading them well into the paste. Repeat the same process with the vanilla and sugar (1 cup at a time).
3. Continue kneading until the dough is firm enough to be rolled into small balls. (Add more sugar if too limp.)
4. Divide the dough into several large balls. Add food coloring to each one before molding into fruits, flowers, animals, and so forth; or shape your candies first and then paint with food coloring.

THE IRANIAN LANGUAGE

Most of the people in Iran speak Farsi or Persian, a language written in the flowing Arabic alphabet. It is an Indo-European language but includes many Arabic words as well.

PRONUNCIATION TIPS

The phonetic guide below closely approximates the Farsi pronunciation:

Vowels
a = ah (father)   e/ea = eh (bet)   i = ee (meet)
o = oh (toe)   oo = oo (boot)   ae/aie = ha (hay)

Consonants
gh = guttural, pronounced in back of throat
kh = a gargling sound

COMMON EXPRESSIONS

Hello	Salam	How are you?	Haleh shoma chetoreh?
Good morning	Sob bekher	Good night	Shab bekher
Please	Khahesh mekhonam	Thank you	Merci
I love you	Man tou ra doost darm	Good-bye	Khoda hafez
What is your name?	Esme shoma cheye?		
My name is _____.	Es me man hast _____.		
How old are you?	Shoma shad salehet hast?		
I am _____ years old.	Man _____ salam ast.		

Numbers

1 yek	4 chachar	7 haft	10 tah
2 tou	5 panj	8 haght	11 yazdah
3 sea	6 sish	9 nough	12 dawazdah

This is my _____.   *len _____ ast.*

mother	madar	sister	khaharam
father	pedar	teacher	moale
brother	baradarm	friend	doost man

JAPAN

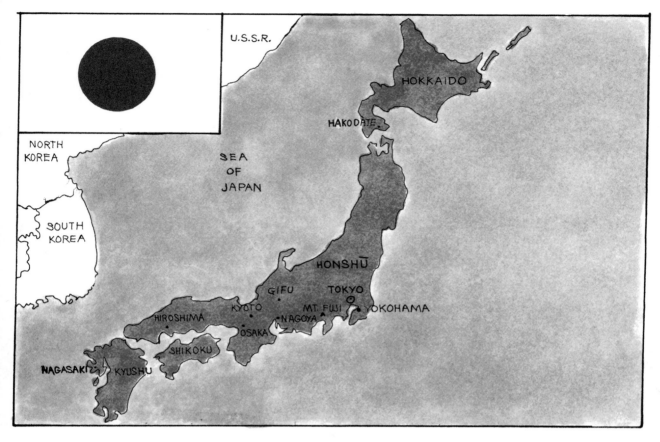

Traditionally called Nippon, or "Source of the Sun"

AREA	145,730 square miles (slightly smaller than California)
POPULA-TION	111,934,000 (1975 est.) (one-half of total U.S. population)
	Largest minority, Korean (less than 1 million)
LANGUAGE	Japanese, official and universal
RELIGION	Buddhism and Shintoism
	Minority religions are Confucianism, Taoism, Christianity
CURRENCY	Yen = .0033¢ About 300 yen = $1.00
PRINCIPAL EXPORTS	iron cars
	steel motorcycles
	textiles ships
	electronic equipment cameras
CLIMATE	Warm to moderate cold; parallels eastern shore of United States from Maine to Florida. The Kuroshio, or Japan Current, causes Japan to be warmer than other countries in the same latitudes; the Great Current, or Oyashio, brings colder weather to the north.

INTRODUCTION

Can you imagine half the population of the United States living in an area the size of California? This ratio of people to space is a fact of life in the tiny island country of Japan . . . and even more amazing is the fact that its one hundred eleven million people are crowded into only *15* percent of the land! Most live in cities and small farms along the coastlines, because the country's interior is covered with mountains, hills and forests. It is said that Tokyo, Japan's capital and the world's second largest city, has less space per person than any city in the world. Ginza, its main shopping center, is as crowded on a Monday morning as Times Square on New Year's Eve and has even more neon lights and movie theaters!

Japan is a land of contrasts — where Old World traditions mix easily with the most modern technology of the twentieth century. Truly a blend of old and new, of East and West: visitors have noticed that the Japanese will race through traffic, then spend an hour preparing a ceremonial tea; at the railroad stations, businessmen can be seen bowing low to one another in greeting before stepping aboard the fastest train in the world; on returning home, these same men in Westernized suits and ties will probably leave their shoes at the doorway before changing into their kimonos.

The people of Japan have successfully combined what they consider to be the best of Japanese and Western ways of life, reflecting each in their choice of food and entertainment. They eat both sukiyaki and spaghetti, and enjoy attending Kabuki theater as much as watching "cowboy Westerns" on television.

The Japanese, of Mongoloid stock, are a homogenous group both racially and culturally, with one unifying language. This background, coupled with the country's history of relative isolation until 1853, has allowed the values handed down for generations to remain unchanged: a great respect for their elders, a quiet courtesy, a love of beauty and simplicity and an enjoyment of nature.

With so much coastline and 1,400 harbors around the four main islands, it is not surprising that Japan is one of the world's greatest fishing countries, supplying one-sixth of the earth's total catch! Japanese fishing boats sail the seas from the Aleutians to Africa, and over sixty-three varieties (2,500 tons) of fish — from tiny sardines to huge tuna — are sold each day at the Tsukhi market on Tokyo's busy waterfront. No wonder Japanese families eat twice as much fish as the people of any other country! An unusual form of fishing takes place in Gifu on the island of Honshū where crowds gather under the light of flaming torches to watch night fishing. Trained birds, called cormorants, are used for this centuries-old custom. Japan's unique method of oyster farming, in which floating crates are used as nurseries for growing oysters, produces more than 200 million cultured pearls each year. An amazing sight is the women oyster divers (*ama*) who plunge to a depth of forty-five feet, with only diving masks and ear plugs for equipment.

Japan has become one of the world's leading manufacturing countries despite a crushing military defeat in World War II. This remarkable economic growth has been stimulated by Japan's technical ingenuity, business know-how, government incentives, and a skilled, hardworking labor force. Exports from Japan have soared in the last decade and now names like Sony, Honda, Panasonic and Toyota are household words. Radios and television sets, cameras, automobiles, motorcycles, ships and textiles (including synthetics and 90 percent of the world's raw silk) are the primary exports, many of which are manufactured by huge conglomerates called *zaibatsu.* Japanese industrialists take great pride in the high quality of their products, always competing to make their nation *sekai ichi,* Number One, in the world.

One of Japan's latest engineering marvels is the 34-mile Seika Railroad Tunnel, the largest ever built. Today passengers traveling from the isolated northern island of Hokkaido can reach Tokyo in only fifty minutes, a trip that formerly took four hours by boat! Perhaps this tunnel will encourage residents of Japan's overcrowded capital city to settle in the "new frontier lands" of Hokkaido. Another example of Japan's modernized transportation system is the spectacular Tokaido "bullet train" which speeds along at 120 miles per hour, leaving behind the modern "skyscrapers" of Tokyo (limited by law to twelve stories because of the threat of earthquakes) for the ancient shrines and gardens of Kyoto.

Many Japanese ideas and customs have been incorporated into the American life-style: *ikebana* or flower arrangement, *sikitei* or rock gardens, *bonsai* trees, *origami, haiku* poetry and Zen . . . all providing Eastern beauty and harmony to blend with our Western ways.

THE JAPANESE HOME

When you walk into a Japanese home, you will immediately sense naturalness and simplicity everywhere. Nothing is overdecorated. A low table and cushions are often the only furniture. The Japanese use the term *shabui,* meaning restrained elegance. They will group only a few "choice" items together, each specifically chosen for its beauty.

Tokonoma

Characteristic of this is the *tokonoma,* the "corner of beauty" (but the little alcove actually can be found anywhere in the living room). A painted scroll hangs on the wall above a platform or low table holding a graceful vase of flowers . . . perhaps a single spray of peach or cherry blossoms.

Try creating your own *tokonoma.* If you have an honored visitor, invite him to sit closest to the *tokonoma.* Of course, he will have removed his shoes before entering the house, pointing the toes toward the street; this will save his host the trouble of kneeling to do it for him later as he is leaving.

The typical Japanese home, built of bamboo, is very small, often with only two rooms, and is heated by charcoal burning in an earthenware pot called a *hibachi.* Decorated *fusuma* (sliding screens made of opaque paper in one side of a wooden frame) separate the living areas from the sleeping areas and woven straw rugs called *tatami* cover the highly polished wood floors. The room size is actually measured by these 6-foot by 3-foot floor mats so a Japanese family might describe their house as having an eight-*tatami* room!

Kakemono

The *kakemono* or hanging scrolls were developed from 1100 to 1300 and told funny, adventurous and historical tales in a series of pictures. Try making one yourself using thick brushes and dark ink for the outlines and soft pastel watercolors for the accents. (Special bamboo brushes, such as the Japanese use, are best for the delicate markings made with the soft brush tip.) Keep your drawings simple; they are meant to look real, but not like photographs.

113

Ikebana

Ikebana, the delicate art of flower arranging, follows three principles: the tallest flower or flowers are "symbolic of Heaven"; Earth always holds the middle position; and Man, the root, is the lowest. *Ikebana* is said to bring all people close to the very essence of nature. In all of their flower arranging the Japanese stress line rather than form or color.

In your own arrangements, you might use real flowers or make them from tissue or crepe paper. Buds represent the future, while full blossoms stand for the past. You may wish to include a chrysanthemum, since this flower, with its sixteen petals, is found on the well-known crest, or *mon,* of the emperor's family. Emperor Hirohito is the one hundred twenty-fourth holder of the title, since the same family has occupied the chrysanthemum throne since the sixth century A.D. Every family has a *mon* or family insignia, which is embroidered on the back of the kimono (called a *monisuki*) for weddings and other formal occasions. If you were to design a *mon* for your family, what symbol would you choose?

Religion

Religion also plays an important part in the Japanese home. In almost every house you will find two altars; one honoring the mystic Kami, god of Shinto, and the other honoring Buddha. The original religion of Japan, Shinto, is also the first religion to come into the life of the Japanese baby since he is usually presented at a local shrine shortly after birth, and officially becomes a member of the community. Shintoism emphasizes nature worship and simple prayer, while Buddhism stresses the unity of body and mind. The two do not conflict with one another but exist side by side. The Japanese strive to have *wa* or harmony at the very center of their lives and to be as one with nature.

Baths

Cleanliness is such an important part of Japanese life that even taking a bath becomes a ritual. If you were a Japanese child, you would fill a deep oval-shaped wooden or porcelain tub with very hot water, and then do the actual washing *outside* the tub! Sitting on a low stool and using a wooden bowl, you would splash water all over your body, not worrying about the mess since there's a drain in the floor. Only after your body is soaped and rinsed thoroughly would you get into the tub.

Family members bathe in a prescribed order; first the father, then the eldest son, the other sons, the daughters and last, the mother. If the tub is large enough, more than one person can sit in it. It's not unusual to find a grandfather and his grandson soaking in the tub together.

Since many houses do not have bathtubs, there are public bathhouses with tubs large enough to accommodate forty people at one time! Because bathing is also a social occasion, much chattering can be heard from the separate men's and women's halls.

Gardens

Most Japanese homes, no matter how small, have some kind of garden; many are outdoors while others are found inside in the form of *bonkei* (landscapes on a tray). The gardens are designed to give a feeling of beauty, harmony, simplicity and calm, and contain only a few basic elements, such as stones, small plants, a few flowers, or a tree or bush. Often a pond or small waterfall is added to create a feeling of space. Fat red goldfish and a low curved bridge add to the picturesque scene. Sometimes a garden might consist of sand raked in swirling patterns banked by a few stones and moss. A famous garden at a temple in Kyoto has only white pebbles and black rocks, yet the simplicity and delicacy in the arrangement make it admired throughout the world. It has been said that the gardens of Kyoto are "like *haiku* poetry come alive."

You might create your own *bonkei* to keep in your home or school. Start with a shallow dish or pan filled with dirt or sand. Keep your arrangement uncluttered, perhaps a delicate plant flanked by a few moss-covered rocks or a small mirror to give the effect of a miniature pond.

A more ambitious project would be to transplant a seedling to a clay pot and practice the art of *bonsai,* the cultivation of dwarf trees. Choose a hardy seedling (pine, fir, oak), pinch back some of the branches, and using wire, train the others to bend into interesting positions. Place the tree in a sunny spot and water it often.

The Japanese take pride in their *bonsai* trees. Many, more than one hundred years old, are passed down from generation to generation. Brushing some of the dirt away from the top of the roots will give your *bonsai* tree an ancient look.

FESTIVALS

Japan is truly a land of festivals. The Japanese word for festival is *matsuri* and there are *matsuris* celebrated in every part of the islands. Many are religious and historical; others are just "special" days.

Shogatsu (New Year's Day)

Shogatsu is the favorite holiday in Japan when according to an old Japanese proverb, everything gets a new start. At midnight on December 31, bells toll 108 times to remove all the evils of the past year . . . and on New Year's Day (*Ganjitsu*), January 1, *everybody* has a birthday! Families celebrate by decorating their homes, sending elaborate handmade greeting cards, visiting friends and paying off personal debts. Girls wearing gaily colored pajamas play a type of badminton called *hanetsuki* while boys fly kites and spin tops. Every child *must* have a new kimono to wear during the holiday season.

During this happy time, it is customary for the family to gather for a festive meal at which the special food served is called *mochi* or rice cakes. These were traditionally made by the man of the house pounding the steamed rice and the woman then shaping it into the small round cakes. The Japanese drink *toso,* spiced *sake,* to toast good health, an ancient custom handed down from China. *Shogatsu* lasts for fifteen days and the holiday closes with the burning of the *kadomatsu,* a traditional decoration or wreath made of bamboo and branches of the plum and pine trees.

Outside Heian, the famous Shinto shrine in Kyoto, boys and girls buy fortunes scratched on white paper and tie them, like blossoms, to the bare-branched trees to bring good luck.

Take a look at the calendar and make a list of all your classmates who have birthdays during the summer months when there is no school . . . then you could have a *Ganjitsu* party and celebrate all of the birthdays together. Maybe you can even make a "fortune tree" or decorate some *hanetsuki* paddles!

If you were in Japan at *Shogatsu* time, you might want to compete in the emperor's annual contest for the best amateur poet!

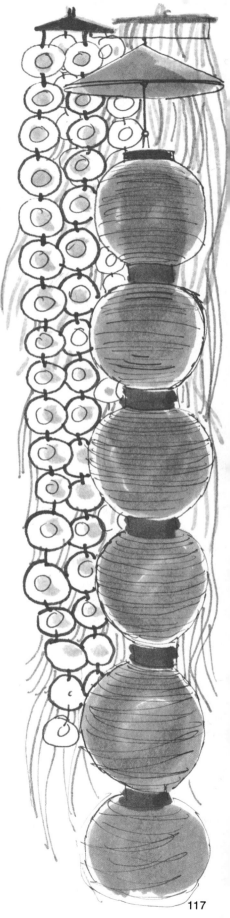

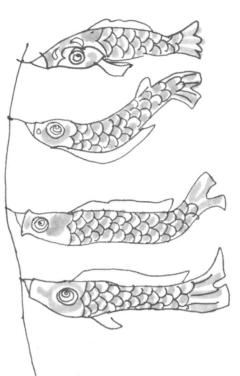

Tonge-no Sekku (Boys' Festival)

Perhaps the next most exciting day in Japan is the Boys' Festival on May 5. Tall bamboo poles appear in front of *all* the houses where boys live. At the top are brightly colored banners (made of cloth or paper), one banner for each boy in the family.

Each banner is in the shape of a carp. This symbol is selected because the carp is a fish so strong and brave that it can leap a waterfall and parents hope to see these same qualities in their sons. How many fish will be "flying" in your classroom? In your home? On your street?

In later years this festival has been expanded to include the girls and is now called Children's Day or *Kodomo-no-Hi.* The paper carp are still flown for the sons, but the real purpose of the holiday is to impress on all children the importance of being good citizens, and courageous and strong at all times.

Hina-Matsuri (Doll Festival)

A very special day for all the girls in Japan is March 3, the date of the Girls' Doll Festival. This is when the girls display their collection of ceremonial dolls, which have been passed down to them for many generations. These decorative, ornamental dolls are arranged in a special order, with the emperor and empress on the highest shelf. The girls often visit from house to house admiring one another's dolls and exchanging sweet cakes and rice wine. Afterward the dolls are returned to their silk wrappings and lacquered boxes for another year.

You might have your own Doll Festival at home or at school. Invite your friends for tea and ask them to bring their favorite dolls. Display all the dolls on a colorful tablecloth surrounded by peach blossoms made from paper . . . in Japan, the peach blossoms are always in bloom at festival time!

A favorite treat served at the Doll Festival is an "Orange Blossom Basket."

Cut oranges or tangerines in the shape of baskets (see picture), being careful to scoop out the fruit inside *without* breaking the handle. Fill with orange-flavored gelatin and bits of fruit and place in the refrigerator until firm. Save the rest of the fruit for a salad or mix with sherbet for dessert.

Tanabata

Tanabata is the festival of the stars. It celebrates an old Chinese legend that says that "on the seventh day of the seventh moon the boys' star lying on one side of the Milky Way and the girls' star on the other meet at the Milky Way." On that day tall paper lanterns are hung in the streets with Japanese letters pasted on the front and strings of colorful beads and crepe paper tied to the bottom. Use construction or crepe paper and clay beads to make your lanterns.

Still today on *Tanabata,* Japanese children erect a bamboo tree and write poems on rice paper or colored paper to hang from the tree. (It is said that the children take the first dew of the morning off a lotus leaf to dilute the ink for writing their poems.) Many Japanese schools set up displays of poetry written by their students, and families decorate their doorways with poems.

RICE PAPER

Surprise your family or friends by writing a story or poem on rice paper! To make your own paper: arrange flower petals, leaves or thin twigs on gray construction paper and cover with a piece of white tissue paper. Brush lightly over the tissue paper with a solution of white glue and water, continuing until the tissue paper is thoroughly saturated. (This should result in a little lumpiness!)

Let the "rice paper" dry, then write or paint some original *haiku* poetry on it.

HAIKU POETRY

The *haiku* is a short, nonrhyming poem that suggests a mood or picture, often a season of the year. It contains seventeen syllables and usually three lines:

    First Line — the setting of the poem (5 syllables)
    Second Line — the action of the poem (7 syllables)
    Third Line — the conclusion or feeling (5 syllables)
    Example: A day in July
               Colorful kites are flying
               Soaring high above.
Tanka is a five-line poem with the syllabic pattern of 5, 7, 5, 7, 7.

KIMONOS AND FANS

The traditional Japanese clothing for the Doll Festival and other special occasions is the kimono, a one-piece, loose-fitting garment with wide sleeves; it is folded over in front and held together by an *obi,* or sash. The designs on the kimono are symbolic of Japan's four seasons. When a Japanese girl becomes seven years old, she puts on her first stiff *obi.*

The special holiday dress for boys is a short kimono (the girls' are ankle-length) with a wide, divided skirt called a *hakama.* Both boys and girls can wear a kimono-shaped cloak or *haori* over the kimono.

Design your own kimono with an *obi* and try to find the appropriate footwear for the occasion. Japanese children wear *geta* (wooden clogs) or *zori* (rubber or straw sandals), as well as *tabi,* socks that have a separate place for the big toe and are worn with the *geta* or *zori.* You might improvise with heavy cardboard and yarn to make a similar thong-type sandal.

Fans would add a decorative finishing touch. Here are three different Japanese-type fans for you to make.

1. For a simple, *flat* fan, cut a piece of cardboard or Styrofoam into a round or oval shape; insert it between two tongue depressors or in a slit cut in a cardboard tube (the Japanese themselves would use bamboo). Glue in place and wrap colored tape or contact paper around the handle.

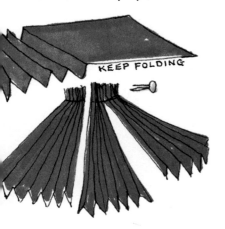

2. *Folded* fans were invented in Japan over twelve hundred years ago to brush the flies away from the sacred vessels in the temple, and also for use in ceremonial dances. It is said that the inventor may have determined how to fold his fan by noticing how a bat folds its wings. For this fan, fold three sheets of construction paper either into one large semicircle (held together at the bottom by a staple or brads) *or* with one overlapping the other (vertically), leaving a two-inch border at the top.

121

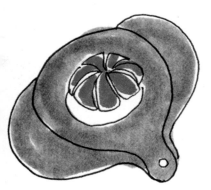

3. The Japanese use a special *three-bladed* fan as a platter to serve tea cakes. Cut out three "light bulb" shapes from heavy paper or thin cardboard and join them at the bottom with a brad fastener.

Use crayons, paints or markers to decorate your fan, or cut a "snowflake" pattern out of colored paper and lay it over a paper of another color. Tassels tied to the bottom will give all of your fans a decorative touch. It might be fun to choose your own special design. For example, the seventeenth-century *Mai Ogi* (Dancing Fan) showed the family crest popular among the aristocrats, while other fans had historical figures painted on them. A seascape would surely be appropriate, since wherever you go in Japan, you will never be more than seventy miles from the sea.

TEA CEREMONY (Chanoyu)

The tea ceremony was brought to Japan from China in the seventh century by the Zen Buddhists. It is still today a time for silence, meditation and rest, when the mind can concentrate on harmony, respect, purity and tranquillity.

It takes years of study and practice to learn the many steps of the *Chanoyu* ceremony but few achieve the "master of tea" degree, a ten-stage process. Even though you have not had this special training, you can follow some of the authentic Japanese rituals in serving tea to your guests. They might follow the old tradition of bringing an extra pair of *tabi* to change into because of the "dusty" roads along the way.

First bow to your guests to welcome them and invite them to kneel on the small, low cushions, or *zabuton,* which you have provided. You would call

your friend by his last name, always adding the word *san,* a term of affection (John Smith would be Smith-san).

The tea ceremony is formal and follows a set pattern; each step is a miniature experience in its own right.

1. First serve your guests a small rice cake or sweet from a piece of rice paper, while you prepare the utensils.

2. Clean the ladle (*chashaku*) with a red silk napkin.

3. Wipe the rim of the pottery bowl (*chawan*) with a special white linen cloth.

4. Warm the *chawan* with hot water and dip in the bamboo stirrer (*chasen*) to rinse it. Pour out the water with a *chashaku.*

5. Scoop the finely powdered green tea (*ocha*) from a lacquered box into the *chawan.*

6. Ladle the boiling water into the bowl and stir vigorously with the *chasen* until the tea foams.

7. Turn the bowl one and one-half times around (the most decorative part of the bowl is always turned toward the guest and no one drinks from that side) and serve the first guest, who out of respect asks the others, "May I drink first?"

8. The guest bows and then takes three sips while inhaling deeply. After the first sip the hostess asks if the guest likes the tea and, of course, the guest always says, "Yes." On the last sip, it is polite to make a slurping noise to please the hostess.

On a warm day, you might enjoy a less formal "picnic tea" outdoors, served on a bright red cloth spread on the ground. A special treat to Japanese children, which you could include in your tea ceremony, is *kanten* (gelatin blocks).

KANTEN

YOU NEED:

1 6-ounce (177.4 ml) can frozen
  fruit juice
4 envelopes unflavored gelatin
1 cup (240 ml) cold water
6-ounce (177.4 ml) package orange
  gelatin
1 cup (240 ml) sugar
4 cups (960 ml) boiling water

YOU DO:

1. Soften gelatin in the cold water.
2. Dissolve sugar and orange gelatin in boiling water and then add the fruit juice and gelatin solution, mixing well.
3. Place in a 9" x 13" pan and refrigerate. Slice into blocks after hardened and serve.

JAPANESE THEATER

The Japanese people have made many great contributions to the arts. In addition to poetry and paintings, they are known for music, particularly the Suzuki Method of playing the violin, and for theater. Their two traditional forms of theater, the Noh and the Kabuki plays are admired the world over.

Noh

The Noh plays started as ancient poetic dance-dramas, actually combinations of chanting, music and dancing. In today's presentations, the chorus chants the story while the actors slowly dance and pantomime. Many of their movements are symbolic: a few steps forward mean a journey, hands to face signifies weeping, and so forth.

The actors wear special masks, each representing a different emotion or character. These masks are said to have long traditions and are carefully preserved, along with the beautiful costumes. Can you make a mask expressing joy? Sorrow? Anger? Fright?

If you decide to reenact a Noh play in your classroom, don't worry about scenery. The actors generally perform on a *bare* stage with a *hanamishi* (runway) leading to the dressing room. There might be a painting of a lone pine tree in the background to remind the audiences that the Noh plays used to be performed outdoors. Try to include some drums, a high-pitched flute and a zither for background rhythm. The Japanese would probably add a *koto,* a horizontal harp, and a *samisen,* a lute. Also, instead of presenting one long continuous play, you might duplicate the Noh method of giving four or five short ones.

Kabuki

The Kabuki theater, which followed the Noh plays, is much faster-moving. The name Kabuki means "leaning to one side" or "being playful." In contrast to the historic Noh dramas often played for the aristocrats, the Kabuki was said to give the ordinary people what they really wanted! Even now the stories are often based on family scandals and horror stories. The Kabuki, considered to be quite melodramatic, has had a great impact on its audiences. Men traditionally take all the roles, even though the law banning actresses was repealed years ago. The man who plays the role of a woman in these plays is called *onnagata;* actors also play the parts of horses, foxes, dogs and demons. The best of the Kabuki plays were written by Chikamatsu Monzaemon, often called the Shakespeare of Japan. In his plays he stressed the merit of honorable behavior.

Planning a Kabuki-style play will take much more preparation than the Noh, since it is a skillful combination of color, acting, music and costumes. Some of the elaborate costumes weigh as much as fifty pounds, including heavy wigs!

Stage makeup, or *kumadori,* will play a very important part in your production; stark white signifies the role of a woman; bright lines of color, the hero. White, red and black makeup is still used in the Kabuki to create the effect of power and strength. Be sure to arrange for a *hanamishi* right in the middle of the audience. About six feet wide, it extends from the stage all the way to the rear of the auditorium so the players can interact with the audience.

Finally, you will need wooden clappers to beat together while the actors are performing. The clappers are particularly noisy when the curtain opens, lending a tone of dramatic excitement to the theater.

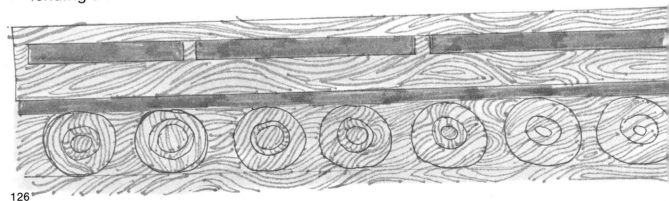

Bunraku (boon-rah-koo) — Japanese Puppet Theater

Another traditional type of drama, which once rivaled the Kabuki, is the Bunraku Puppet Theater in Osaka. While the art of puppetry in Japan dates back one thousand years, this particular theater is descended from an even earlier one that was founded by Uemura Bunrakken in the early ninth century.

Bunraku puppets do not have strings. Each puppet, about two-thirds life-size, is manipulated by three men, standing in full view of the audience. Two are dressed all in black, including black hoods over their faces, while the principal operator wears a brightly colored jacket and high stiltlike shoes. The garb of the puppeteers could be distracting, but the puppets appear so real that the audience soon forgets that the three men are even there! To heighten the dramatic effect, the heads of the puppets have movable eyes, mouths and eyebrows. Their words are spoken by a "chanter" who sits to the audience's right on a big cushion placed on a revolving platform. The chanter projects his voice like a ventriloquist and sobs and makes gasping sounds that are highly exaggerated, as are the puppets' gestures and movements. Next to the chanter is his musical accompanist playing the *samisen*. Music plays a very important role in the Bunraku Theater and guides all three components — the puppets, the operators and the chanters — enabling them to work together in harmony and keep the play flowing smoothly.

STAGE YOUR OWN BUNRAKU
PUPPET THEATER

Make your puppets with papier-mâché heads (see p. 145) and cloth bodies; or an even simpler way would be to cut them from cardboard, using brads to connect the joints. Remember, Bunraku puppets are very large and so you will need to figure out what two-thirds of your own height would be in order to design a puppet of your own age. Since many of the Kabuki plays were originally written for the Bunraku, the features of the two are similar. Just as in the Kabuki, the Bunraku chanter begins the play by beating wooden clappers together and reciting the names of the "cast." His call of "tozai" (hear ye) signals the samisen player to begin.

To learn the art of operating Bunraku puppets takes years of training and the skills are handed down from father to son. One operator manipulates the puppet's feet, the second, the left arm, and the third, or chief, operator works the puppet's right arm and head. It takes more than twenty years before a puppeteer can become a principal operator, for he must spend ten years just moving the feet, and ten more years working the left arm!

Few props are used in a Bunraku theater in order to leave room for the three operators. Do you think you could move all of the parts of a Bunraku puppet with two of your friends and avoid tripping over one another? Try it and you will soon appreciate the fine art of Bunraku.

GAMES

Karuta

Poetry is so much a part of everyday life in Japan that a card game called *Karuta,* or "One Hundred Poems," is one of the most popular ones. It is traditionally played by families on New Year's Day; you might find three generations sitting on the floor all participating in the game, as Japanese families have done for eight hundred years.

Choose a leader to read the opening half of a well-known poem from a card; whoever matches the card with the other half of the poem (among the many spread out on the table) gets to keep it. The player with the most cards at the end of the game is the winner. (Sometimes in Japan, the leader will chant the opening half, in the style of a praying monk.)

Most of the Japanese games, however, are based on ancient legend. Two of these are *Fuku Wari* and *Rakan San.*

Fuku Wari

This game also is played at New Year's time. On a large sheet of paper, draw an outline of the head of Otafuku, goddess of fortune, coloring in only her hair. Tape the paper to a door or wall. From another sheet of paper, cut out eyebrows, eyelashes, eyes, ears, nose and a smiling mouth. (Rolled-up masking tape on the back of each feature will make it stick.) Each child, blindfolded, tries to place a feature on Otafuku's face.

Otafuku is always smiling. Her motto is "laugh and grow fat!"

Rakan San

Rakan is an ancient Buddhist priest who supposedly had an odd-looking face.

Players sit or stand in a circle, each facing slightly toward the person on the right so one can *observe* that person's actions. First everyone takes a pose. Then all chant together, "Let us all imitate a *Rakan* pose. *One, two, three,* POSE."

This time each takes the pose of the player on the *right!* As the game continues, change poses and go faster.

Jan Ken Po

The next game, *jan ken po* (scissors, paper, stone), which is well-known to children in many lands, originated in Japan. The Japanese children often use it for settling a tie.

jan (scissors)	*ken* (paper)	*po* (stone)
middle & index	*hand held flat*	*clenched fist*
fingers extended		

The game is played in pairs. Each player counts to three as he pounds his fist three times against the palm of his hand. Then he must form the sign of *jan, ken* or *po* and a winner is determined as follows: scissors cut paper; paper covers stone; stone breaks scissors.

Another favorite game is one using beanbags. The child flips them from the palm to the back of the hands, first with both hands, then with only one. Make your own beanbags by sewing together small squares of material or using the toes of old socks, filling them with dried beans, rice or pebbles.

Crab Race

Since Japan leads the world in crab fishing, it is not surprising that another popular game in Japan is a "Crab Race."

To play this game, form two relay teams and set up goal lines. The first player in each line leans backward, and moving on all fours (to resemble a crab), progresses to the goal line and back. The player then touches the next player who continues in the same fashion.

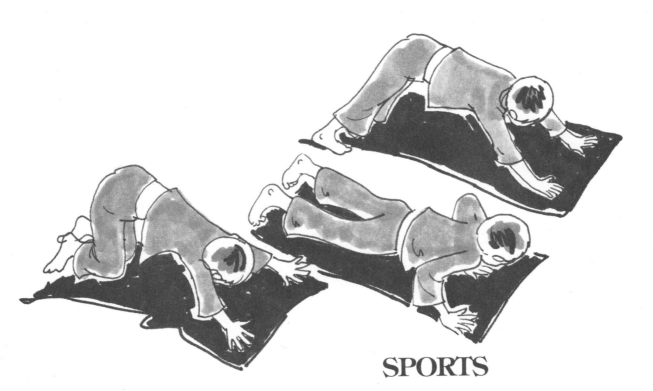

SPORTS

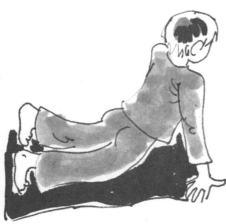

In addition to their enjoyment of games, the Japanese are enthusiastic sports fans. Tickets for *Sumo,* a form of wrestling, are said to be as hard to get as World Series tickets in the United States! Japanese children not only enjoy *Sumo,* but also judo and karate, often as "spectator" sports. Karate, which means empty hands, is a style of fighting by jabbing, hitting and kicking with elbows, hands and feet to the cry of *"Kiai!"* It is so dangerous that when boys are learning, they practice it on wood and tile instead of on each other. As their skill increases, the open fist can break a plank of wood or even a brick! Karate is held under strict controls by the Japanese police who allow only holders of special permits to practice this sport.

Baseball has become Japan's national game. However, soccer, football, basketball, volleyball, tennis, hockey, swimming, and now even skiing have joined the list of favorite sports. The Japanese take their sports seriously and are traditionally competitive, always striving to keep fit and to use proper clothing and equipment.

Japanese children also spend their leisure time flying kites, spinning tops, playing *ayatori* (cat's cradle), making plastic models and bicycling.

TOYS AND CRAFTS

Japan is the home of the largest toy industry in the world. One of the country's best-known folk toys is the *daruma*.

Daruma

The *daruma* is constructed so that whenever it is pushed over, it always lands in an upright position. This is symbolic of Dharma, legendary founder of Zen Buddhism, who stressed the importance of acquiring an inner serenity and a balanced and orderly daily existence.

Simple ways to make a *daruma:*

1. Paint the *daruma*'s face on a paper cone and then set the cone, pointed end up, into a clay base; or

2. Draw the face on heavy paper, and using a toothpick, insert in half an orange rind filled with clay. Be sure to give the base enough weight so it will "right itself" when tipped.

One of the most charming traditions associated with this folk toy is the "wishing" *daruma* made without eyes. When a child makes a wish, he paints in one eye, and the *daruma* is given his second eye only after the wish has come true!

Children in Japan also build snowmen in the shape of the *daruma*. If you live in a cold climate, you might try fashioning a *daruma* in the snow.

Kokeshi

Another traditional toy (over three hundred years old) is the *kokeshi* doll, a wooden cylinder with a painted ball on top, which makes a sound like a baby crying when the head is turned. You could make a *kokeshi* from a cardboard tube and a rubber, Styrofoam or Ping-Pong ball.

Origami

A very popular craft project, closely associated with the Japanese, is *origami,* the art of folding paper (*ori* means fold and *gami,* paper). It is thought to have originated in China in the seventh century and then to have been brought to Japan, where it was incorporated into the Doll Festival. The children would make paper dolls and throw them into a river to drive away the evil spirits. Even today it is said that a folded paper crane or tortoise attached to an important gift sends a wish for good fortune and long life. It is fun to fold butterflies, animals and fish in such a way that they will appear to be flying . . . or swimming . . . or gliding. Try this *origami* bird.

A Bird

1. Fold a paper square in half to form a triangle.
2. Fold top corner (*c*) down so that the point extends past the baseline of the triangle.

3. Lift up top flap of corner *c.*
4. Fold in half, from *a* to *b.*

5. Fold back one wing to dotted line; turn over and fold other wing.

Japanese children are particularly quick at paper folding but with practice your fingers will fly through the steps as theirs do. Using pieces of round paper, try folding a simple flower pattern.

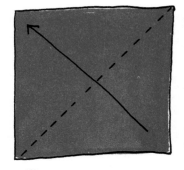

134

While doing *origami,* the Japanese child is encouraged to improvise and invent her own folds. For example, she might take the first two steps in the bird fold and then make an animal face as follows:

An Animal Face

1. Same
2. Same
3. Turn up corners *a* and *b* to form ears.
4. Color or paste on eyes, mouth, whiskers to look like any animal you'd like. Add spots for a leopard, stripes for a tiger, and so forth.

What new shapes can you create?

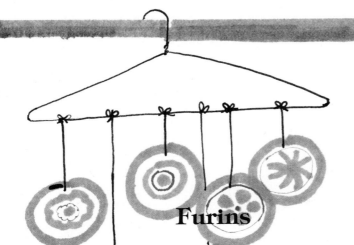

Furins

Japanese *furins* are wind chimes made with glass pendants. They're fun to hear and see.

Why not glue brightly colored construction paper strips around plastic lids and then dangle them from a string? You could also use cookie cutters, six-pack rings or small foil pans for your chimes. Paint your designs directly on the lids, just as the Japanese did on glass. Or if you use a cookie cutter or six-pack ring, glue brightly colored tissue paper or cellophane in the openings. Attach all the pendants to a coat hanger, cardboard tube or wooden dowel, and hang your *furin* in front of a window.

FOOD

The Japanese feel that food should please the eye as well as the palate, and usually serve their food on trays, with each course in separate small bowls to emphasize its unique color, texture or design.

Soup is drunk from bowls; *sake,* Japanese rice wine, is often served in special thimble-sized cups called *sakazuki;* and, of course, chopsticks (*haishi*) are used instead of knives, forks and spoons to pick up the food, which is cut into tiny bite-sized morsels and served in small portions.

Rice and fish are basic foods in Japan. The rice is moist, often flavored with sugar, vinegar and salt, and shaped into rectangles; these rice cakes are then served with shrimp, lobster, tuna or some kind of meat. Meat is cut into thin strips and fried, while fish is often served raw. Garden vegetables are cooked *very* quickly to retain their freshness.

Typical meals served in the village might include one of six varieties of seaweed and bean curd salad and fish and mushroom soup. Pumpkin, cucumber blossoms and chestnut leaves are also combined with fish in one dish! You might try making *tofu,* a bean-curd cake made from ground and jellied soybeans and sold in small squares looking very much like custard. It is often mixed with vegetables and sometimes cooked with fish, meat or soup.

TOFU

YOU NEED:
- 1 15-ounce can green beans or 1 pound (453 g) cooked fresh green beans
- 2 tablespoons (30 ml) sesame seeds
- 1 teaspoon (5 ml) sugar
- pinch of salt
- 1 2-inch cake of *tofu*

YOU DO:
1. Drain and chill the beans (and put aside).
2. Brown the sesame seeds in a frying pan on medium heat for two minutes, turning constantly with a spatula. Pour seeds into a bowl and let cool before crumbling them between your fingers.
3. Add the *tofu* (carefully draining first), sugar and salt and mash the ingredients together.
4. Spoon the *tofu*-sesame mixture over the beans and lightly toss.

Tofu might be served along with *sunomono* (vinegared dishes).

SUNOMONO

YOU NEED:
- 2 cucumbers, peeled (leaving a little skin for color)
- 2 carrots, grated
- 5 to 6 cooked shrimp, cut in bits
- 2 teaspoons (10 ml) salt
- ½ cup (120 ml) rice vinegar (or use white vinegar)
- ½ cup (120 ml) sugar

YOU DO:
1. Cut cucumber into paper-thin slices and mix with grated carrots, shrimp bits and salt.
2. Combine vinegar and sugar and pour over the salad. Stir well and chill.

Tempura and Teriyaki are two Japanese specialties now enjoyed throughout the world. Tempura and other fried dishes were brought to Japan by Portuguese seafarers in the sixteenth century.

TEMPURA

YOU NEED:
- 1 egg, beaten
- 3 tablespoons (45 ml) flour
- ⅛ teaspoon (5/8 ml) salt
- 1 tablespoon (15 ml) water
- 1 carrot, cut into thin pieces
- 1 small onion, cut into wedges
- ½ cup (120 ml) parsley sprigs, long stems removed
- ½ cup (120 ml) salad oil for deep frying
- soy sauce

YOU DO:
1. To prepare the batter, combine the egg, flour, salt and water, mixing until smooth.
2. Heat oil in a saucepan and keep hot over a medium heat. (Test with a drop of batter in the oil; batter should brown quickly.)
3. Drop clusters of carrots, onions and parsley sprigs, one at a time, into the batter and then slide them into the deep, hot oil with a tablespoon.
4. When golden brown, remove them with a fork and drain on brown paper.
5. Serve with a small dish of soy sauce for dipping.

Remember the light touch of the Japanese cook and do not make your fried foods greasy!

TERIYAKI

YOU NEED:
- ½ cup (120 ml) soy sauce
- ⅓ cup (80 ml) sugar
- ½ cup (120 ml) *sake* (dry sherry or white wine may be substituted)

YOU DO: Combine all the ingredients and use as a marinade for chicken and meat to be served with rice. Remember, don't empty your rice bowl unless you are finished, for a few grains left mean "more rice, please!"

Traditionally, Japanese desserts are very light and refreshing. All of the following are easy to make and tasty as well.

FRESH PINEAPPLE WITH ALMOND CREAM

YOU NEED:
- 2 envelopes unflavored gelatin
- 2 cups (480 ml) water
- 2 cups (480 ml) milk
- ¾ cup (180 ml) sugar
- 1 teaspoon (5 ml) almond extract
- 1 fresh pineapple, peeled and cut into cubes

YOU DO:
1. Dissolve the gelatin in ½ cup cold water.
2. Heat the rest of the water with the milk and sugar and add the gelatin and almond extract, mixing well.
3. Pour into a 9-inch square cake pan and chill in the freezer or refrigerator until well set.
4. Cut the pudding into 1-inch cubes and serve along with cubes of pineapple.

Note: For individual servings, you could make the gelatin in small bowls and serve with pieces of pineapple on top.

GREEN TEA ICE CREAM

YOU NEED: 1 pint (480 ml) vanilla ice cream (softened)

1 tablespoon (15 ml) green tea powder

YOU DO: Blend the ice cream and tea powder together, freeze and then serve with a topping.

THE JAPANESE LANGUAGE

Although the basic Japanese language when spoken is entirely different from the Chinese, the Japanese have borrowed from the Chinese in their system of *writing*. The sounds of the Japanese language are written in syllables called *kana* (fifty in number) that are combined with the complex Chinese characters called *kanji* to clarify them. A Japanese student must master 1,850 *kanji* before graduating from high school!

PRONUNCIATION TIPS

Vowels and Consonants
a = ah   e = eh   i = ee   o = oh   u = oo
g has a hard sound.
All of the words end in vowels or the letter n and the verbs come at the end of the sentence.

The following method of writing the Japanese language is called "Romanization" (Latin letters):

COMMON EXPRESSIONS

Hello	Konnichiwa	How are you?	Ikaga desuka?
Good morning	Ohayo	Good night	Oyasuminasai
Please	Dozo	Thank you	Arigato
I love you	Watashi wa anata	Good-bye	Sayonara

What is your name?	Anata no namae wa nandesoka?
My name is _____.	Watashino namae wa _____ desu.
How old are you?	Anatawa ikutsu desuka?
I am _____ years old.	Watashi wa _____ desu.

In Japan adults are always addressed by "san" and children, "chan"; both are terms of politeness. Examples: Kaoru san (adult), Taro chan (small boy) and Mia chan (small girl).

Numbers

1 ichi	4 shi	7 shichi	10 ju
2 ni	5 go	8 hachi	11 juichi
3 san	6 roku	9 ku	12 juni

This is my _____.   *Kore wa watashinō ——— desu.*

mother	*haha*		*sister*	*shimai*
father	*chichi*		*teacher*	*kyōshi*
brother	*kyōdai*		*friend*	*tomodachi*

NIGERIA

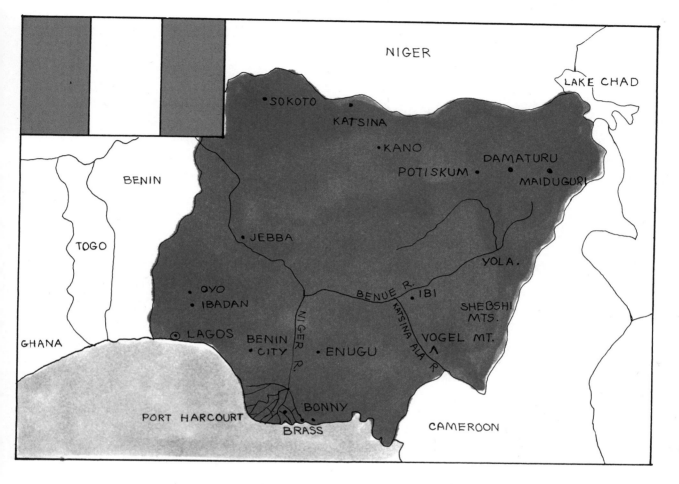

Official Name: Federal Republic of Nigeria

AREA	379,628 square miles (Texas and New Mexico combined)
POPULA-TION	81,800,000 (1975 est.) (four times the population of California)
LANGUAGE	English is official language 250 African languages; most widely spoken are Hausa, Yoruba, Ibo and Edo
RELIGION	47% Moslem 34% Christian 19% Animist
CURRENCY	Naira (.623 naira = $1.00)
PRINCIPAL EXPORTS	crude petroleum palm nuts cocoa rubber peanuts raw cotton
CLIMATE	Tropical

INTRODUCTION

In today's world, Africa can no longer be thought of as a remote "dark continent." Nearly all of her countries, once under colonial rule, are now independent nations. Nigeria, the largest in population (almost 81 million in 1976) is a leading African power. In and around the cities of Nigeria, you will find skyscrapers, supermarkets, modern highways, and even hamburgers and Coca-Cola . . . and yet there are villages in the isolated bush areas of the country where natives living in grass and mud huts have never seen or heard of any of these modern features.

Because of its central location on the coastline of western Africa, Nigeria has for centuries been a crossroads for travelers moving throughout the continent. This is why the country has so many different kinds of people. A close look at Nigeria's history reveals hundreds of years of turmoil with internal tribal warfare and outside invaders constantly changing the makeup of the people. Prior to 1485 no white man had set foot on Nigerian soil. Then for the next four hundred years many Europeans, the Portuguese being the first, came into the country in search of slaves. The British rule of Nigeria, which began in 1848, lasted until 1960, when Nigeria claimed her independence. The Federal Republic of Nigeria was officially established in 1963.

Given Nigeria's location and history, it is not surprising that today there are within its borders 250 tribal groups speaking as many different languages or dialects. Welding together a mixture of tribes — Hausa, Yoruba, Ibo, Fulani, and hundreds of others — has not been easy without the common bonds of religion, race or cultural traditions. Each citizen has had to put aside tribal loyalties and customs in order to develop a primary allegiance to the nation . . . to think of himself as first and foremost a Nigerian. In one effort to unite the people, English has been made the official language, and Universal Primary Education (U.P.E.) now guarantees every

Nigerian child a free elementary education. Perhaps this line from the Nigerian national anthem sums up the country's hope for the future: "Though tribe and tongue may differ, in brotherhood we stand."

Nigeria is the size of Texas and New Mexico combined. When you look at the map, you will see that the Niger River and its tributary, the Benue, form a Y shape that divides the country into three regions. The *northern region,* bordering the Sahara, has had a strong Moslem tradition since the thirteenth-century Arab invasion. The largest tribe is the Hausa, whose alphabet is written in Arabic characters. Every Moslem city has at least one mosque; the most famous one in Kano is an impressive white building with a blue dome and four white minarets (pointed towers) at the corners. Kano is the world's largest exporter of peanuts. On its docks you can see huge pyramids of peanuts, each built of over 10,000 sacks of shelled nuts, a cargo so valuable that it is kept under guard twenty-four hours a day.

The *western region* was the first to be exposed to European ways and therefore was most affected by Christianity. The largest tribes in this area are the urbanized Yorubas. Ibadan, with its great university, and Benin are the key cities. The major seaports, industries and oil centers are concentrated in the *southern* part of the area, including Lagos, Nigeria's present capital and largest city.* Located on an island, Lagos is a federal district similar to the District of Columbia. Cocoa is the leading crop, while tropical fruits and vegetables (bananas, pawpaws, cassavas and yams, the most popular staple) grow abundantly in the wet climate near the equator.

The *eastern region* is known for the energetic, hardworking Ibo merchants, often called the "shopkeepers of Nigeria." Thick, tropical rain forests where rice, mahogany and royal palm trees grow profusely are characteristic of the region. Hippopotami, monkeys and parrots inhabit the coastal swamps, while baboons, elephants, leopards, gorillas, civets, antelope, gazelles, hyenas and lions

*Because of heavy traffic congestion, by the turn of the century, Nigeria will have a new capital city in the center of the country.

roam freely . . . and lizards, lizards, and more lizards! But one animal you'll never see in Nigeria, or in all of Africa, is the tiger.

These three diverse regions combine to form the progressive twentieth-century Nigeria whose influence, along with that of her West African neighbors, is being felt around the world. In the United States there is widespread interest in African culture, which leads to a natural interest in Nigeria.

ARTS AND CRAFTS

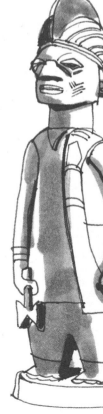

Nigeria is a storehouse of priceless art treasures. In the old walled city of Benin there are museums containing some of the finest bronze and ivory carvings the world has known; terra-cotta figures dating back to the sixth century, found buried in the sand of the Jos Plateau by Yoruba tin miners, are now on display there, along with magnificent ancient bronzes. Bida is famous for wood carvings and handsome metal bowls and trays. It is not unusual for a workman unexpectedly to come upon an ancient artifact when digging a foundation for a new house or road.

The tradition of producing beautiful handmade crafts continues throughout modern Nigeria. "Petty traders," usually women, travel all over northern Africa selling tie-dyed and woven clothing and carved calabashes. At a very early age, Nigerian children begin to work side by side with older members of their families to create these attractive, yet practical, items.

Calabashes

Decorative calabashes are particularly well-known in Oyo, where the carvers make these plentiful gourds into musical instruments, beads, bowls, water jugs, covered dishes, spoons, and other everyday utensils. Women even dip their fingers into long calabash bowls filled with red dye . . . a fashionable "home manicure!" Calabashes grow on vines like pumpkins or watermelons. When ripe, the soft insides are scooped out and the hard rinds are left to dry in the hot Nigerian sun. A carver might work a whole day on only one container, etching complicated geometric designs into the outer shell with a sharp metal tool. Often the gourd is blackened first with wood soot and grease, which is then carved away, leaving light-colored outlines.

Since growing a calabash is impossible on our continent, you could substitute papier-mâché when making your decorative pottery.

1. Cut or tear newspapers into narrow strips.

2. Blow up several balloons (use various shapes, depending upon what you want to make).

3. Cover part of each balloon with five or six layers of paper strips, dipped one at a time into a mixture of white glue and water. (Slide each strip through your thumb and fingers to remove the excess liquid.)

4. Dry overnight and sand the rough edges, if you wish. With a pin, burst the balloon and remove it.

Now you are ready to paint or stain your "calabash" (Nigerians often use shoe polish) and then scratch a design on it. (Use a knife or nailhead.) Finally apply a finishing coat of shellac both inside and out.

Papier-Mâché Ceremonial Masks

Nigerian masks, representing their ancient gods, have exaggerated features such as bulging eyes, protruding noses, prominent lips and teeth and pointed fangs. You can use the papier-mâché method to create authentic-looking African masks. After the mask is painted and shellacked, carve out the features and then add yarn, feathers, raffia, and other decorative touches.

A very quick and easy method for making a mask is to attach a stick to a paper plate, adding on parts of egg cartons, paper cups, or small cardboard boxes for three-dimensional facial features. Paint with bright colors and glue on beads, aluminum foil cutouts, crepe-paper curls, and so on.

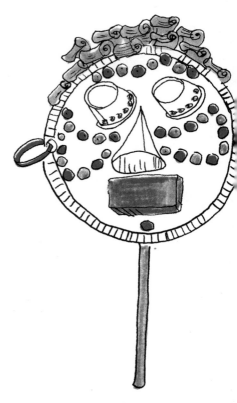

Adire Eleso (Tie-Dyeing)

Adire is a Nigerian tie-dyeing process used to create beautiful patterns on cloth. The city of Kano, in northern Nigeria, is famous for its dye pits, and particularly for a deep blue dye made from the fermented leaves of the indigo plant, which grows wild in the area. The dye is poured into holes that are dug ten feet into the ground and surrounded by thick clay rims. Workers, shaded by straw umbrellas, spend hours dipping hand-woven cloth into the dye and stirring it with long bamboo poles until it turns the desired tone. Blue is a popular color for Nigerian clothing because it cuts down the glare of the intense sun. Bright oranges, greens, yellows and browns are also used.

146

For your own tie-dyeing:

YOU NEED:
- a broomstick cut into several pieces or a thick dowel rod
- old sheets
- plastic bags
- old buckets, tubs, or dish pans
- clothesline
- heavy string
- dye

YOU DO:
1. Wrap a piece of material over the stick, tying it tightly at intervals with string. (Strips of plastic bags tied tightly around the banded areas will help resist the dye.)
2. Dip the tied cloth into the dye solution, keeping in mind that the longer it soaks the deeper the color will be.
3. Cut the strings and remove the cloth from the stick. Then rinse the cloth in cold water, dry on a clothesline and press with a warm iron.

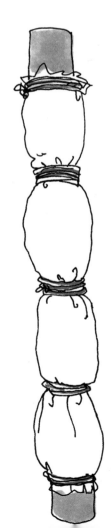

(In Kano, the dried cloth is then set over a log and pounded with a mixture of butter and glue, giving the cloth a special sheen.)

Note: If you are using more than one color, begin with the lightest one and work your way to the darkest, repeating the first four steps before adding each new color. Remember to tie off each color area you want to "save" before dipping into a new color.

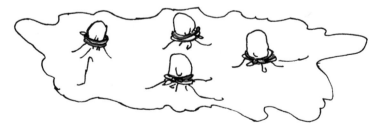

Another Method of Tie-Dyeing
Spread out a piece of material (T-shirts and pillowcases can also be used). Pull up small sections into "peaks" and secure with rubberbands. The peaks can be placed at random or in a particular design. Then follow Steps 2 and 3 above.

Of course, the most exciting part of the tie-dyeing is when you finally open the cloth and see the original patterns that *you* have created.

NIGERIAN FASHIONS

Now that you have made your own beautiful tie-dyed cloth, you're ready to create a traditional Nigerian outfit. While the style and trim, and even the names of the garments, will vary from tribe to tribe, the basic costume for men and women is a simple shirt and a long, free-flowing robe. Because of the hot climate, the clothing is designed for comfort with loose-fitting sleeves and skirts.

Dashike

YOU NEED: material
scissors
needle and thread

YOU DO:
1. Fold a rectangular piece of material into fourths.
2. Cut openings for the neck and sleeves.
3. Add a facing to the neck; then hem the sleeves and bottom, or finish off the edges with an embroidery or slip stitch.

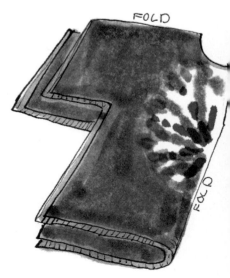

Many Nigerian men wear a short *dashike* over a pair of pants, while both men and women may choose a longer version falling below the knees. Members of the Moslem Hausa tribe generally wear several full-length white robes with wide billowing sleeves . . . it is said that the more gowns a Moslem wears, the wealthier he is.

The Yoruba variation of the *dashike* is called an *agbada* (poncho) and is worn with baggy trousers, or *sokotos.* Fulani women wrap a cloth around their bodies as you would a bath towel; the men wear a short gown with tight pants, hand-embroidered at the cuffs, which end just below the knee. The Bush tribes deep in the remote areas of Nigeria may wear only a band of fresh leaves tied around the waist, while the chief wears a single brightly colored sash, which designates his rank.

Lapa

To make a *lapa,* a Yoruba woman's skirt, wrap a hemmed length of cloth one and one-half times around your hips and tie at the waist. With her *lapa,* the Yoruba woman may wear a scoop-necked blouse called a *buba,* along with a large sash called an *iborun.* A heavier sash called an *oja* is used to carry a bundle or even a baby, keeping it close to its mother as she goes about her daily chores.

If your tie-dyed material isn't wide enough, you can sew together several strips of cloth to make any of these Nigerian gowns.

Beads

Nigerians like to adorn themselves with many necklaces, bracelets, earrings and anklets. To complete your outfit you can make your own African beads. Sequins, buttons or clay beads can be strung on plastic thread in any sequence or pattern.

To make the clay beads, mold small pieces of clay into any shape, then string on heavy wire to dry or to be baked. They can be painted and shellacked or glazed and fired, depending on the type of clay. You can even make papier-mâché beads to resemble those made from chunks of calabash.

Hats

Nigerians wear a variety of hats and hairstyles. A favorite is the huge, broad-brimmed, woven straw hat extending over the shoulders to provide shade. Some are cone-shaped with leather tips and chin straps; others, worn by the Fulani, have rounded tops with wavy brims.

Brightly patterned turbans are elaborately wrapped around the head, each fashioned differently. The Yoruba women call theirs *gele,* for which they use a cloth two yards long and twelve to fifteen inches wide. They place the center of the cloth at the back of their heads and bring the two ends forward and around to the back again, tying and tucking in any loose ends. Some Hausa women wear turbans with long trains of fabric that they can pull across the lower part of their faces like a veil. The Moslem man may shave his head and wear a white turban.

The Yorubas have a small pillbox-shaped hat with a tassel that they wear at a jaunty angle. You might make yours from a tall round food container (from ice cream or cottage cheese or the like). What will you use for a tassel?

Hairstyles

Nigerian men and women spend hours creating intricate tribal hairdos. Rows of little braids (sometimes mixed with twists and bunches) form unique patterns. Many people rub their hair with pomade to make it shiny. The Kanuri in the north have an unusual custom: unmarried ladies pull all their hair into a topknot, while married women wear the same hairstyle but dangle an additional pigtail over their foreheads. Fulani women wear a bun on top and weave brass ornaments into pigtails that they arrange over their ears. Why don't you experiment with some of these hairstyles?

BEAUTY SHOPPE

Body-Painting

Another form of tribal decoration is body-painting, still in use today, particularly for ceremonial rites and holidays. Body and facial scarring, once a custom of tribal identification, is no longer used except in the remote bush areas. Older tribal members, however, can still be easily recognized by their decorative incisions.

MARKETS

Bustling outdoor markets where you can buy everything imaginable, from soap to camels, can be found all over Nigeria. Opening early in the morning, they continue until the hot sun is setting. A common sight along the Niger and its many tributaries is canoes and houseboats jammed together to make floating dockside markets.

The best-known city market, located in Kano, began as a thriving marketplace for desert caravans. To reach Kano, the sellers even today may travel one hundred miles or more, by oxcart or, like the Fulani herdsmen, by riding cattle, while still others travel via huge lorries or "mammy wagons" that sway under the weight of the dozens of riders and goods crowded inside. These brightly painted vans, many driven by women, collect "shoppers" from remote, out-of-the-way places, stopping at every local village and farm. Many people bring their products to market on foot, balancing woven baskets, calabash bowls and trays on their heads. Today a Hausa trader might even arrive on a bicycle with his wares tucked under one arm.

An air of excitement pervades the marketplace, with its varying smells and sounds. Drummers and musicians wander through the crowds playing for a "tip." There are rows upon rows of stalls and booths packed with an enticing assortment of fresh produce, aromatic spices, precooked snack foods ("small chop"), colorful clothing, handsome leatherwork, and jewelry, as well as wood, brass and ivory carvings. The food stalls feature everything from fiery red peppers to smoked monkey ribs, antelope meat and dried crocodile meat! There is much bargaining between buyer and seller and *everyone* is talking at once. Often village children, carrying their stools and books on their heads, stop at the market on their way home from school to buy *chin chin* or *akara* (a cake made of black-eyed peas and fried in oil), both favorite snacks.

Plan your own Nigerian market and make posters to announce the time and place of this special event. Each seller needs an area to spread out his wares. A Hausa trader would use a straw mat, but you might substitute a towel or blanket. Some "merchants" could sell *dashikes, lapas* and *geles* created from their own tie-dyed fabrics as they do at the Blue Market at Ibadan. Set up a stall to tempt your buyers with typical Nigerian dishes.

FOOD

The food of Nigeria, like its crafts and music, is a reflection of the regional diversity of the country. Most Nigerian families usually eat two meals a day . . . once early in the morning when it is cool and again in the evening when the sun is setting. They refer to their main meals as "chop" and to their snacks as "small chop." A favorite "small chop" often eaten during the course of the day is *chin chin.*

CHIN CHIN

YOU NEED:
- 2 tablespoons (30 ml) butter
- 1 cup (240 ml) flour
- 2 teaspoons (10 ml) sugar
- 1 teaspoon (5 ml) caraway seeds (or nutmeg, anise, or grated orange rind)
- 1 beaten egg
- vegetable oil for deep frying (have an adult help with this)

YOU DO:
1. Knead the butter and flour together thoroughly, then add the sugar and caraway seeds.
2. Mix in the beaten egg to form a stiff dough. (A few drops of water may be added, if needed, but the dough should be kept firm.) Knead until smooth.
3. Roll out on a floured surface and cut into strips (about ½ to ¾ inches wide by 4 to 5 inches long) with ends cut on a diagonal.
4. With the tip of a knife, make a small slit just left of center and slip the righthand end through it, forming a little loop.
5. Heat the oil to 350° to 375° F (180° to 190° C) and fry each *chin chin,* turning with tongs to brown evenly.
6. When they are crisp and brown, remove from oil and drain on paper toweling. Makes about three dozen pieces.

The peanut, called "ground nut" by the British, is as common among Nigerian children as bubblegum or popcorn is with Americans. You might want to try "Ground Nut Soup" or a stew called "Ground Nut Chop."

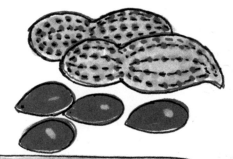

GROUND NUT SOUP

YOU NEED:
- 1 pound (453.6 g) shelled roasted peanuts (place peanuts in a pan and heat in a 350° F — 180° C — oven for 30 to 40 minutes, turning occasionally)
- 6 cups (1440 ml) beef or chicken broth
- ⅓ cup (80 ml) chopped onion
- 1 to 2 cups (240 to 480 ml) cups half-and-half (half milk, half cream)
- 1 tablespoon (15 ml) cornstarch
- salt to taste
- red pepper to taste
- parsley or chives

YOU DO:
1. Grind nuts very fine.
2. Heat the broth, add nuts and onions and bring to a boil, then simmer for 1 hour, stirring occasionally.
3. Press mixture through a sieve or beat in a blender and return to the pan.
4. Mix milk with cornstarch in a small bowl, stirring until smooth. Stir 2 tablespoons of the soup into this mixture, then add the entire mixture to the soup.
5. Add seasonings and continue simmering for 30 minutes.
6. Sprinkle on parsley or chives for a festive garnish.

GROUND NUT CHOP

This is a favorite main dish that can be served with any of the following side dishes: peanut butter, sliced oranges, bananas sprinkled with lemon or lime juice, sliced tomatoes, green peppers, cucumber, fried onion rings, toasted coconut, diced pineapple, roasted peanuts, ground red pepper or chopped fried okra. This recipe is for *20 people.*

YOU NEED:
- 10 pounds (4536 grams) stew beef or chicken cut into cubes
- 8 onions, sliced
- 2 teaspoons (10 ml) salt
- 1 pound (453.6 grams) peanut butter
- 1 teaspoon (5 ml) crushed hot dried red pepper
- 2 large cans of tomatoes
- 12 hard-boiled eggs, chopped

YOU DO:
1. Put meat cubes in a large soup pot, add two of the sliced onions, and salt.
2. Cook over moderate heat, letting the meat brown as the juices evaporate.
3. Add enough water to cover meat and simmer 15 minutes.
4. Mix peanut butter with some of the hot broth to make a smooth paste.
5. Gradually add paste to meat, stirring all the time.
6. Add pepper, tomatoes, the rest of the onions and the chopped eggs.
7. Boil for 20 minutes.
8. Reduce heat, cover and simmer for 45 minutes.
9. The stew may be thinned out with more water, if necessary.

Nigerians work in their gardens and fields cultivating okra, eggplant, onions, tomatoes, rice, cassava, pumpkins and yams, an important staple food.

FRIED YAMS

YOU NEED:
- 3 yams or sweet potatoes
- 1½ cups (360 ml) peanut or vegetable oil for deep frying. Set aside 2 tablespoons (30 ml)
- salt and curry powder to taste
- 1 sliced tomato
- 1 sliced onion

YOU DO:
1. Peel and slice the yams.
2. Heat the oil and gently drop in the yams, frying until golden brown.
3. Drain and set aside.
4. Fry the remaining ingredients in the remaining 2 tablespoons (30 ml) of oil and pour over the fried yams.

RICE FOO FOO

A favorite dish is rice *foo foo,* which can be served by itself or with a main course.

You may want to substitute cornmeal for the flour, as the Hausa tribe does.

YOU NEED:
- 2 cups (480 ml) hot water
- 1 teaspoon (5 ml) salt
- 1 cup (240 ml) rice flour

YOU DO:
1. Bring 1½ cups of the water to a boil and add the salt.
2. Sprinkle in the rice flour, turning the mixture rapidly with a flat wooden spoon to prevent lumps.
3. Lower the heat and stir for 20 minutes until the rice swells and stiffens.
4. Add the remaining hot water, if necessary.
5. Press the rice *foo foo* into a small wet mold, then turn out onto a platter and serve with butter, salt and pepper.

Fresh fruits, which grow abundantly, such as mangos, pawpaws, papayas and pineapple, have always been standard fare. They are peeled and served on a platter with lemon or lime juice and honey drizzled over them. Nigerian children enjoy sipping refreshing fruit drinks like this spicy homemade pineapple punch.

PINEAPPLE PUNCH

YOU NEED:
peelings from one pineapple
4 whole cloves
4 cups (960 ml or 1 L) water
¼ cup (60 ml) sugar

YOU DO:
Boil water and peelings for 10 minutes, add the seasonings, strain and chill.

Sometimes the parents will pour a few drops on the floor before serving, in remembrance of their ancestors who have passed away.

Although Nigerians did not originally eat a dessert course, the British introduced *their* recipes for baked fruits and puddings, which have become favorite "after chops."

BAKED BANANAS

YOU NEED:
ripe, but firm, bananas (one per person)
brown sugar
crushed peanuts
lemon juice
cream

YOU DO:
1. Set the oven at 350° F (180° C) and bake the bananas in their skins for 20 minutes.
2. Then peel them and sprinkle on lemon juice and brown sugar.
3. Pour on cream and add crushed peanuts . . . delicious!

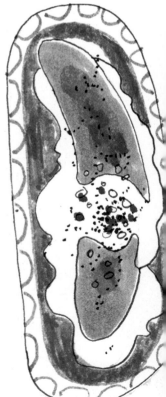

MUSIC

Music is a very important part of any African's life. For centuries it has been a means of communication between one native and another; it has also provided the rich, rhythmic beat of tribal ceremonies. But more than that, music is part of everyday work. All laborers — farmers, fishermen, camel drivers, hunters and soldiers — have "work songs." Natives sing for rain, for good luck or to welcome a new visitor. Birth, marriage, death or a successful hunt are also occasions for a song. Even gossip is circulated through singing!

The "praise singer" plays an important role in various celebrations in northern Nigeria. He mingles among the people, hoping a naira or two will come his way as he sings about the beauty, talent or bravery of a particular guest. Who could resist such compliments? Take turns being a praise singer and make up flattering songs about your family or friends.

Instruments

Africans can make music from anything! Their instruments are divided into four categories: drums, idiophones, aerophones and chordophones.

NIGERIAN TALKING DRUM

IGBIN DRUM

Drums

Drums, called the "heartbeat of the continent," are the most important instruments. It is said that an African is born, lives and dies with the sound of the drums. They come in many sizes and some are even six or seven feet in diameter, resounding for miles.

The Nigerian Talking Drum (*iya-ily*) is a tapered two-headed drum, wide at the top and narrow at the bottom, each end producing a different sound. It can imitate tones of the human voice and even its rhythm.

The *Igbin Drum* is a short, fat drum with only one head.

You could borrow some drums similar to these from your music department or create them from household materials such as mixing bowls, carry-out chicken containers, pails, cigar boxes or ham cans for the base. The drumhead or "skin" can be made by stretching canvas, khaki, oilcloth, chamois, heavy plastic or rubber over the top. Fasten the skin securely with several layers of heavy tape or twine, or twist wire around the rim. If the cloth skin begins to sag, dampen it and let it dry so that it will shrink back to its original tautness and tone.

For a simpler version, find containers with lids — coffee cans, powdered drink cans, margarine tubs, oatmeal cartons, and tennis ball or potato chip cans. Beat the drums with your hands or for drumsticks use eraser-tipped pencils or sticks wrapped at one end with felt.

Idiophones

Idiophones are any instruments that vibrate when struck or shaken.

The *Slit Gong* is a hollow instrument carved out of mahogany or ebony — the larger the log, the lower the tone. What tools would you use to make a slit gong?

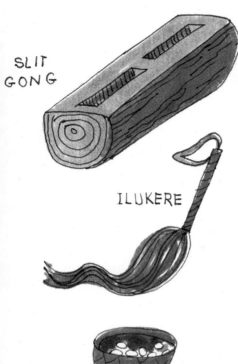

SLIT GONG

ILUKERE

SHAKERS

The *Thumb Piano* (*mbira*), the second most popular instrument next to the drum, is now made from umbrella spokes fastened to a wooden board. By putting screws in a wooden bar to hold the spokes in place, the spokes can be adjusted to change the tone.

The *Ilukere,* made of hair from a horse's tail, with the end wrapped in leather, creates a swishing sound. Make yours from raffia or crepe-paper strips taped at the ends to form a handle. (The *ilukere* is also used very effectively as a flyswatter!)

Shakers can be bells attached to an ankle or wristband, or gourds and woven baskets filled with stones, seeds or cola nuts. You could use tin cans, Band-Aid boxes or papier-mâché shakers filled with bottle caps, dried beans or rice.

Rhythm sticks are pairs of objects knocked together — hollowed-out coconut halves, lacquered wooden sticks or two notched sticks which when rubbed together make a grating sound.

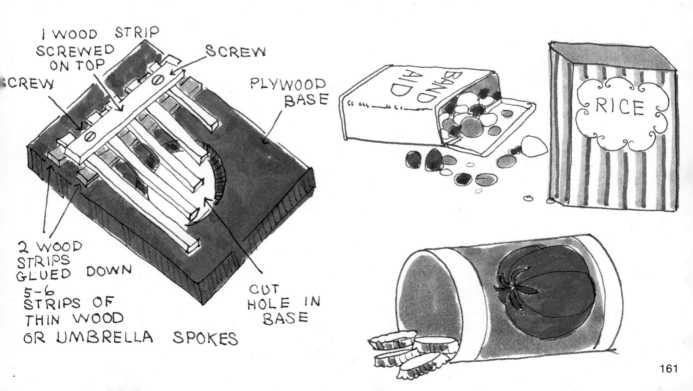

1 WOOD STRIP
SCREWED ON TOP

SCREW

SCREW

PLYWOOD BASE

2 WOOD STRIPS GLUED DOWN

5-6 STRIPS OF THIN WOOD OR UMBRELLA SPOKES

CUT HOLE IN BASE

BAND AID

RICE

Aerophones (Woodwinds)

Whistles and flutes are carved from balsa wood or bamboo, or made from clay. Nigerians use elephant tusks and horns from antelopes, elands and gazelles for trumpets, and even shells produce a beautiful tone. Perhaps you could borrow some whistles, flutes or recorders from your music teacher . . . maybe you could even get a sound out of a seashell!

Chordophones

Chordophones are stringed instruments that are struck, plucked or bowed.

The *Nigerian Harp Guitar,* an eight-string instrument made from a calabash with an animal skin stretched over it, is played by holding one of the guitar's two handles while strumming with the other hand. You could make your "guitar" from a plastic or papier-mâché bowl.

A *Wishbone Harp* consists of a rubber band wrapped several times around each end of a wishbone.

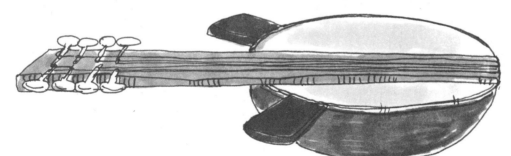

Drumbeats

The drumbeat is the key to African rhythm. Try these authentic Nigerian drum patterns with the drums that you have made. First divide your group into two parts. Using eight beats as the basic rhythm, one-half of the group taps on even beats, the other on the odd, keeping up a steady pace.

Once you've mastered this simple pattern, try a random sequence; for example, one group comes in on 1, 3, 7 and 8, the second group on 2, 4, 5 and 6. Listen to each drum separately and decide which is high and which is low. Regroup according to pitch and repeat these two patterns.

Now divide into at least four groups and using the same eight beats, follow this staggered sequence in which each group starts and ends on a different beat.

Group I	1	2	3	4	5	6	7	8		
Group II		1	2	3	4	5	6	7	8	
Group III			1	2	3	4	5	6	7	8
Group IV				1	2	3	4	5	6	7	8

Can you hear the crescendo building . . . and then fading out?

If you've made a variety of instruments, group them by category — chordophone, idiophone, and so on; practice the previous patterns and experiment with some new ones like this (you may need á "conductor" to bring each section in at the right time):

1	2	3	4	5	6	7	8
idiophone	idiophone					idiophone	idiophone
chordophone			chordophone			chordophone	chordophone
		rattle			rattle		
aerophone			aerophone				
drum		drum		drum			

You can even practice these patterns without instruments — clapping your hands, slapping your thighs, snapping your fingers and stamping your feet. Whatever Nigerian patterns you choose, it helps to concentrate; perhaps count to yourself in order to keep the beat. With practice this can become as natural for you as it is for Nigerian children.

West African Song and Dance

Making music Nigerian-style is fun because it's spontaneous. Since songs and dances are seldom written down, Nigerians make up new variations — improvise — as they go along, never performing the same way twice. Typical of this is "Everybody Loves Saturday Night," which easily lends itself to improvisation. Here are the words and music to this popular song.

Everybody Loves Saturday Night
(Sung with much drumming throughout)

EV–RY BO–DY LOVES SATURDAY NIGHT

EV–RY BO–DY EV–RY BO–DY EV–RY BO–DY

EV–RY BO–DY EV–RY BO–DY LOVES SATURDAY NIGHT

First sing the song together to learn the words and tune. Then choose a leader to sing each line, while the group responds in different ways, perhaps just repeating the line or making comments of agreement or disagreement, or bringing in instruments. The leader might even change the basic verse a bit.

Example:

Leader: Everybody loves Saturday night.
Group: Yeah, man! (Oh yes!)
Leader: Everybody
Group: Are you sure?
Leader: Everybody
Group: You know it!
Leader: Everybody
Group: He's right, man!
Leader: Everybody
Group: Everybody
Leader and Group: Everybody loves Saturday night.

Other variations:
Leader: Who do you know that loves Saturday night?
Group: Mamie does, Annie does, Jason does, etc.
Leader: Ain't nobody loves Mon — day morning, etc. etc.

In African music you'll find no "onlookers." This "call and response" pattern — chorus answering leader — encourages everyone to join in the singing!

The "High Life"

Nigerians also improvise *dance movements* to their favorite songs. The contagious sound of "Everybody Loves Saturday Night" quickly brings people to their feet to dance the "High Life." With or without partners, often in a circle, young and old alike shuffle in time to the music — hips wiggling, shoulders shaking and head nodding. Put on *your* "dancing shoes"!

West African Music and American Jazz

West African music with its steady rhythm, expressive dialogue and spontaneous improvisation laid the foundation for American jazz. First came the blues, the mournful laments of the Negro slaves on the plantations, which were a direct imitation of the West African work songs. The earliest jazz music grew out of Negro funerals, the only occasions when slaves were permitted to sing in public. A slow, sad hymn could be heard on the way to the graveyard, but a joyous spiritual like "When The Saints Go Marching In" often followed the mourners home. Even though they were forbidden to use the drums and percussion instruments they brought over from Africa, some slaves managed to make them in secret, improvising with washboards and whatever else they could salvage. The American jazz movement is greatly indebted to the early slaves who kept their African music alive.

STORYTELLING

Storytelling is an old tradition in Nigeria. Families often gather in their compounds in the evenings listening for hours to folktales that have been passed down from father to son for generations. The qualities of humor, fantasy and exaggeration give these stories universal appeal. Some are about superstition and magic or how the world came to be; others have frightening or violent themes; some describe heroes and tricksters; and many are fables with animals as the leading characters, a favorite among them being the tortoise known for his wisdom. Most of the tales have a *moral* at the end, much like this one.

A Nigerian Fable

The chief sent out messengers to announce that he would give a feast and asked each guest to bring one calabash of palm wine. One man wanted very much to attend, but had no wine to bring. When his wife suggested that he buy the wine, he said, "What! Spend money so that I can attend a feast that is free?" He thought to himself, "If hundreds of people were to pour their wine into the chief's pot, could just one calabash of water spoil so much wine?"

The day of the feast came. Everyone bathed and dressed in their best clothes and gathered at the house of the chief. There was music and festive dancing. Each man, as he entered the chief's compound, poured the contents of his calabash into a large earthen pot. The man also poured his water there and then greeted the chief.

When all the guests had arrived, the chief ordered his servants to fill everyone's cup with wine. The man was impatient, for there was nothing so refreshing as palm wine. At the chief's signal, all the guests put the cups to their lips and tasted . . . and tasted again . . . for what they tasted was not palm wine but water! *Each* guest had thought his *one* calabash of water could not spoil a great pot of good palm wine.

Do you know the moral of the story? No doubt you'll think of many different ones!

Group Activities

Group rhythm patterns can add a lively dimension to the storytelling. Assign certain sounds to heighten the drama of each scene. Perhaps a loud drumbeat whenever the chief is mentioned, taps with rhythm sticks as each guest enters, and another sound that would represent the pouring of the "wine" into the earthen pot. African dancers often use parts of their bodies as "instruments" to accompany their dances. You can adapt this to your storytelling by clapping your hands, slapping your chest, clicking your tongue, smacking your lips. If you prefer using rhythm instruments, see page 160.

You might enjoy making up an original folktale, or even trying your hand at a fable with a moral. For an authentic presentation, do as the Nigerian storyteller does. Imitate the characters as you tell the story, and sometimes even act out the scenes. Maybe you could add a tongue-twister to your folktale like this Yoruba favorite: *"Jaguda je gbaguda Aguda"* (The thief ate Aguda's cassava). See the bibliography for other West African folktales. You will note that these were not written down by the Nigerians themselves, but recorded by interested missionaries, travelers and anthropologists who listened to generations of African storytellers.

— At the chief's signal, all the guests put the cups to their lips and tasted...

GAMES

Many of the games popular in Nigeria originated in other parts of West Africa. For instance, *Da Ga,* Moonshine Baby and *Nte-Too* are all from Ghana. Most Nigerian games are played outdoors.

Da Ga (The Big Snake)

One player, chosen to be the *Da Ga,* tries to catch another player. The person caught must join hands with the "snake" and the two of them chase the other players, tagging from either end of the "snake." The *Da Ga* grows longer and longer as each player is caught. Mark off boundaries to limit the playing area.

Catch Your Tail

Players divide into teams and form a chain with the end players dangling a handkerchief or scarf from their pockets or belts. The first in line leads a team in a chase, trying to grab a "tail" from one of the opposing teams. Again, a limited area is recommended.

Moonshine Baby

1. One person is "it" and leaves the area.
2. The others choose a player to be the "Baby."
3. The "Baby" lies down on the ground while the players outline her with stones, sticks or chalk. She then joins the other players. (Be sure to brush her off first!)
4. "It" is called back and tries to guess whose "silhouette" it is. If he guesses correctly, he gets another turn; if not, a new player is chosen to be "it." (Note: This game can be played on the beach using shells or a stick to draw outlines in the sand.)

Nte-Too (Playing with Seeds)

Two players face one another, each kneeling behind his own row of twelve nuts. The first player rolls one of his nuts toward his opponent's line, trying to hit a nut. If successful, he captures the nut and continues. When he misses, the other player keeps the "roller" and takes his turn. The player with the most nuts wins.

Variation: To make the game harder, place the lines farther apart.

Jumping the Beanbag

Players form a circle while one player in the center holds a rope with a beanbag or sack tied securely to one end. As she swings the rope close to the ground, each player in turn must jump over it — or is out of the game. The "swinger" increases her speed each time the circle gets smaller. The last one left is the winner.

Ayo

Ayo is a very old board game still enjoyed throughout Africa, its popularity extending to the Middle East and even to South America. The game is played rapidly, for it is said that "to delay is a violation of the spirit of the game."

Two players sit opposite one another and use a wooden board that has two rows of six cups each, with a "home cup" at each end. Since an egg carton already has the same arrangement, this game can easily be played with an egg carton and two additional containers as "home cups."

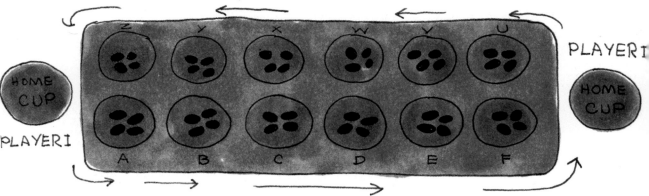

To set up the game:

1. The cups in one row are labeled A, B, C, D, E and F and those in the other row U, V, W, X, Y and Z.
2. Four seeds, pebbles or nuts are placed in each of the twelve cups.
3. One row is assigned to each player and play proceeds in a counterclockwise direction.

To begin the game:

1. Player I moves the four seeds from any of his cups, "planting" one into each of the next four consecutive cups. For example, if he chose Cup B he would then put one seed in C, D, E and F. (Note: *A player may never at any time begin a move from the other player's row.*)
2. Player II does likewise. For example, if she selects Cup X, she would place one seed in Cups Y, Z, A and B.

The game continues in this manner, each player moving *all* the seeds from the chosen cup, planting one in each consecutive cup.

The object of the game is to capture as many seeds as possible from the opponent's cups. Seeds may be captured in two ways:

1. When your *last* seed planted lands in an opponent's cup *already* containing one or two seeds (and no more), you may capture these seeds.
2. Going backward from that last cup, you can collect seeds from all *consecutive* cups containing only two or three seeds.

The game ends when one player has twenty-four seeds in his "home cup" or when neither player has a move. At that point, the player with the most seeds wins.

THE NIGERIAN LANGUAGE

Although the official language of Nigeria is English, the three major ethnic groups, Hausa-Fulani, Ibo and Yoruba, speak their own languages. The one used here is Yoruba.

PRONUNCIATION TIPS

Vowels and Consonants

a = ah	e = a (bait)	ẹ = e (pet)	i = e (wet)
o = o (go)	ọ = a (all)	u = oo (too)	p = kp

The above or below a letter indicates different pronunciations and meanings of certain Yoruba words that are spelled alike.

COMMON EXPRESSIONS

Hello	Pele	How are you?	Se da da ni?
Good morning	Karo	Good night	Odaro
Please	Jọwọ	Thank you	A dupe
I love you	Mo feran re	Good-bye	Odabo

What is your name?	Kini orukọ re?
My name is _____.	Oruko mi ni _____.
How old are you?	Ọmọ ọdun melo ni ọ?
I am _____ years old.	Ọmọ ọdun _____ ni mi.

Numbers

1 ōkan	4 ẽrin	7 ẽje	10 ẽwa
2 ẽji	5 ārun	8 ẽjọ	11 okanla
3 ẹta	6 ẽfa	9 ẽsan	12 ẽjila

This is my _____.		*Eyi ni* _____ *mi.*	
mother	iya	sister	antí
father	baba	teacher	olùkọ́
brother	ẹ̀gbọ́n	friend	òrẹ́

SOVIET UNION

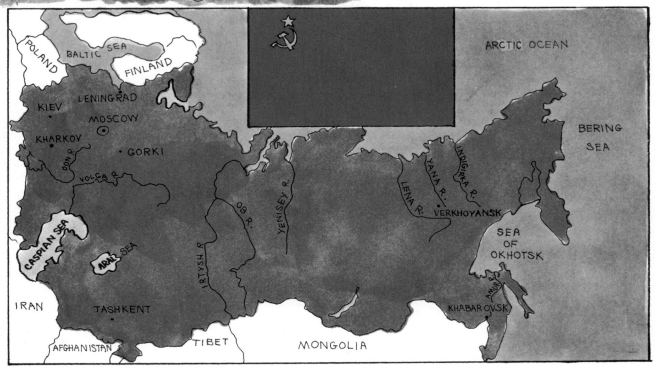

Official Name: Union of Soviet Socialist Republics

AREA	8,647,250 square miles (over $\frac{1}{7}$ of all the land on earth, nearly 2½ times the size of the United States, not counting Alaska and Hawaii)
POPULATION	254,380,000 (1975 est.) (slightly more than the population of the United States)
LANGUAGE	Russian is official language — spoken by 60% of the population as a first language. Other languages — Ukrainian, Belorussian, Lithuanian, Latvian and about 60 more
RELIGION	Russians and Ukranians: 18% Orthodox. Central Asia: 9% Moslem. Other: 3% Roman Catholic, Protestant, Jew, Buddhist. Atheism is officially propagated by the government, followed by 70%
CURRENCY	1 ruble = 75¢. 100 kopecks = 1 ruble
PRINCIPAL EXPORTS	machinery, foodstuffs, iron, lumber and paper products, steel, textiles, crude oil
CLIMATE	Cold, known for its long, bitter winters; short, but hot or warm summers

173

INTRODUCTION

The Union of Soviet Socialist Republics, known as the Soviet Union and often referred to as Russia, is the largest country in the world. Spanning two continents, Europe and Asia, the Soviet Union stretches over 6,000 miles from east to west, almost two and one-half times the size of the United States. In fact, the country is so vast that a jet airplane could take off from Domodedovo Airport in Moscow, head east, fly for eight hours and still land within the Soviet borders (at the city of Khabarovsk on the Amur River)! Five of the world's longest rivers are located in the Soviet Union, including the Volga, a river made famous by the "Song of the Volga Boatmen." Seventy million people live and work along the banks of this mighty river, the longest in Europe (2,300 miles).

There are no simple characteristics typifying the Soviet land and people. If you look at the map of the Soviet Union, you will discover desert regions, as well as rugged mountain peaks, forests, highlands and flat plains. Most of the country lies in the same latitude as Canada and has the same range of climate — from cool-temperate to frigid. Verkhoyansk, on the Yana River, is considered the coldest place on earth outside the Antarctic.

The Soviet Union is made up of fifteen republics and more than one hundred nationality groups, each with its own language, dress and traditions. It's truly an ethnic patchwork, from the Laplanders living with their reindeer in the north, to the dark Armenians on the southern border of Turkey, from the blond, fair-skinned Slavs in the west, to the dozens of mixed Mongol groups in the east.

The largest of the nationality groups is the Slavs, which includes the Russians, the Ukrainians, the Armenians, the Georgians, and so on. These people are primarily Caucasians and make up three-quarters of the population. The largest of the non-Slavic groups are the Turkics, descendants of the

Turkic tribesmen, many of whom married the invading Mongols from the land lying north of China.

There is more farmland in the Soviet Union than in any other country, and wheat is the chief crop. Nearly 30 percent of the Soviet people are engaged in farming, with millions more recruited from the cities each year to help at harvest time. However, farming is difficult because of the periodic droughts. In an attempt to convert an agricultural country into an industrial power, the Soviet government has pursued a series of Five-Year Plans since 1928. As a result, the Soviet Union now leads all countries in the production of coal, iron ore, manganese, lumber and petroleum.

All aspects of Soviet life are controlled by the government — not only the farmland and the factories, but the newspapers, schools, libraries, museums, department stores and even the circuses! If you were a child living in the Soviet Union today, you'd have few options regarding your school subjects or recreational activities and your parents would have even less flexibility in choosing their occupations. Not many families have a television set and even fewer have cars. Most people live in crowded conditions because housing construction cannot keep pace with the steady migration of people from the country to the city.

On the other hand, the standard of living is slowly improving with the average peasant now earning approximately ninety-eight rubles a month, or $73.50, as compared with $1.80 less than fifty years ago (around the beginning of the Stalin era). There is no unemployment, taxes are low, housing inexpensive, and medical care and vacations are available at little or no cost at all. The cities are immaculate, with strict pollution control, and because of the low level of crime, it is safe to walk the streets at night. Moscow's subway, the Metro, is considered by many to be the most beautiful in the world. If you were to

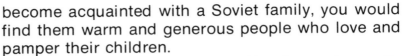

become acquainted with a Soviet family, you would find them warm and generous people who love and pamper their children.

The government places specific demands on its people: that they should live by the standards of the Communist Party and that every citizen — from the youngest child to the oldest grandfather — should work and study for the betterment of the country. Yet, within this rigid framework, the Soviets take great pride in their country's accomplishments. Their outstanding list of authors and playwrights includes Tolstoy, Dostoevski, Turgenev, Pushkin and Chekhov; among the world's most renowned composers are Tchaikovsky, Prokofiev, Stravinsky, Rimski-Korsakov and Shostakovich. The dancers Pavlova and Nijinsky are only two of the many names associated with the "greatest" in ballet, along with Diaghilev and Moisheyev, world-famous choreographers. The Soviets are also internationally known for their important advances in science, sports, space and education.

EDUCATION

Education in the Soviet Union is taken very seriously. To accommodate the working mothers, schools are open from 7 A.M. until 7 P.M. with four hot meals served each day. Children attend school six days a week, and although classes are taught in the local language of the region, the same courses are taught throughout the country. Russian is introduced as the basic language in the second grade. In the fourth grade, when students begin a foreign language, many choose English.

Students wear uniforms to school; the girls, a black or white pinafore or smock, and the boys, dark gray or brown suits with white collars. Once students have joined the Young Pioneers, the Soviet youth organization, they wear bright red kerchiefs with their uniforms.

Classes are highly structured with emphasis on indoctrination into the Communist way of life and on group behavior and discipline. For example, praise will be given not to the individual student but to the *row* that can sit up the straightest. Often discipline is handled by the children themselves. As a typical example, a representative chosen by each class reports on any child's misdemeanors at a school assembly *each morning.* If a child is not working as hard as he should, his penalty is to have his name posted in the factory office where his father or mother works. Parents of young children even receive a printed sheet of procedures to use at home, including what time children should get up in the morning, what they should eat, when they should be bathed and what books should be read to them.

Job Training

To prepare for future jobs, the schools stress science and technology, including industrial skills, both in the classroom and through on-the-job training. A student will work in a nearby factory to learn wood or metalwork, textile printing, and other trades. Around 85 to 90 percent of the students go on to higher education, attending special institutes in agriculture, engineering, medicine, teaching and so on. After graduation all the students work without salary for three years to repay the government for their education.

Children's Railroad

Summer jobs are no problem for teenagers. They are sent to various parts of the country where needed, particularly in August when they can help with the harvesting. A favorite summer job among Soviet young people is to work on the railroad operated by the children themselves. There are at least thirty railroads of this kind, the best known located in a park in Kiev. Here the children run the three stations, ticket office and signal boxes; the only adult is the engine driver. In the winter some of these same children belong to a railroad club and many will choose the railroad as their life's career.

On-the-Job

It's unlikely that you could run a railroad in your community, or even take over a less specialized job. However, if you could *observe* an occupation first-hand to learn about it, which would you choose? Arrange to accompany or "shadow" an adult on his or her job or change places with your teachers, principal or school staff for a day!

Cultural Life

Since the Soviet government is very concerned with the future of the country and the development of educated, talented citizens, there's a great emphasis on culture. Every big city has its own palace of culture, a bustling center of activity open every night of the week for Soviet families to enjoy. There are over nine hundred museums in the Soviet Union, including the Tretyakov Gallery in Moscow, which displays the paintings of Ilya Yefimovich Repin, the Soviet Union's best-known artist. The largest museum is the Hermitage in Leningrad, which was once part of the sumptuous Winter Palace of the czars, and now houses one of the world's finest art collections. The Hermitage contains 14,000 paintings and 12,000 sculptures. Someone has said that if you were to spend one minute viewing each object in the museum, it would require twelve years for a complete tour! The Hermitage, together with the nearby Pushkin Museum, owns the world's largest collection of French Impressionist and post-Impressionist paintings.

Libraries

There are more libraries in the USSR than in any other country, and the largest children's library in the world is located in Moscow. Every Soviet student is supervised by the librarian from the earliest grades on. Each book read is noted on a personal record that follows the student throughout school. This cumulative record indicates each child's interests and often will help determine a boy or girl's future career.

BOOK CHART

Make a chart of the books that you, your classmates or family have read over the past few months. See if you can determine the main interests of each person. It might be fun to use this chart to predict future occupations . . . scientists, doctors, teachers, and so on. You might also make a card catalogue (using a shoebox and index cards) to classify your home or school collection. Remember to have three cards for each entry and cross-file by author, title and "subject." You could also design stickers to represent different subject areas and place these on either your chart or card catalogue for quick identification.

LIBRARY RESEARCH GAME

Divide into teams and give each the same set of questions to research; or each team could make up a list of questions to exchange with another team. Be sure the facts are based on the books in your homemade card catalogue, or the one in your school or public library. (Wouldn't it be frustrating to hunt for information about the 1980 Olympics in Moscow if that event weren't yet included in your reference books?) Which team will be the first to find the correct answers?

SAMPLE QUESTIONS

1. What is Rimski-Korsakov's best-known work?
2. What connection did the Bolsheviks have with Lenin?
3. Why was the "Five-Year Plan" initiated?
4. Who participated in the famous "Kitchen Debate"?
5. What is the most powerful political body in the Soviet Union?

Note: This game is also challenging and fun to play using only the encyclopedia!

NEWSPAPER

Another Soviet largest . . . Moscow's newspaper, *Izvestia* (news), has the largest daily circulation of any newspaper in the world, over eight million copies. It is the official newspaper of the Soviet government. The first newspapers were published in Russia in 1682 at a time when Czar Peter the Great was introducing many Western ways into the country.

If you decide to publish your own newspaper, where will you begin? Perhaps by taking a look at your local newspaper to see what departments are listed in the table of contents. Discuss the topics for each section and then assign staff reporters to cover them:

News	Family Life
Sports	Foods
Features	Comics
Editorials	Special Events
Fashions	Travel

Of course, there's much more to putting together a newspaper than just writing the articles; there's editing, proofing, layout and paste-ups, headline and caption writing, photography, advertising and circulation. How will you print your paper? (By ditto, mimeograph, or photo offset?) How will you illustrate your copy?

You may choose to build one issue of your newspaper around Soviet life today, with students contributing articles about current political events, sports, space exploration, people and personalities, books, art exhibits, and so on. The Soviet papers, such as *Pravda* (truth) and *Izvestia,* would probably not have comic strips, features like "Dear Abby" or stories of "sensationalism." And of course, there would be no advertisements since everything is government-owned. On the other hand, editorials might be very long, often running six or seven columns!

A visit to your local newspaper would make an interesting and informative field trip; also to the library or a large city newsstand to find newspapers from other countries.

HOLIDAYS AND CELEBRATIONS

Of the many holidays celebrated in the Soviet Union, the most important ones are political, such as Revolution Day and May Day.

Revolution Day

Revolution Day, a two-day celebration on November 7 and 8, commemorates the overthrow of the czars in 1917 by the Bolsheviks, who, led by Lenin, renamed their party Communist and their country the Soviet Union. The event is marked with miles of military parades, bright balloons and banners. Soviet boys and girls wave flags as they watch the colorful ceremonies in Red Square in the center of Moscow.

The Russian word for red, *krasnaya,* also means beautiful, and Red Square is truly an impressive sight, even without a parade. At one end of the square is St. Basil's Cathedral with its towers and onion-shaped domes, painted in red, yellow, blue, green and gold designs. It has been described as looking like peppermint candy sticks encircling a pineapple. One entire side of the square is bordered by GUM, the "Macy's of Moscow," the Soviet Union's largest department store; owned by the government, it is decorated with red banners bearing Communist slogans and large pictures of Marx and Lenin. Nearby is the Lenin Mausoleum where there are always lines of people waiting to view the tomb of their beloved leader. The Kremlin — the Russian word for fortress — stands on sixty-four acres surrounded by high walls. It is from the balcony of the Kremlin that Communist leaders make fiery speeches on Revolution Day. Did you know that the Kremlin has several beautiful parks, three cathedrals, a bell tower, museums, palaces, an armory and many watchtowers? The main gateway to the Kremlin is the Spasskaya (Saviour's) Tower, which, when lit up at night, looks like a glowing star.

MINIATURE RED SQUARE

Reconstructing a mini-Red Square or Krasnaya with its unique architecture would make a challenging project! Using a huge box or tabletop as a base, fashion the buildings out of boxes of all sizes, coffee cans, cardboard tubes, and so forth. To make the many turrets and cone-shaped cupolas, you could roll up pieces of construction paper, or use paper cups and margarine tubs. To form the swirling onion-shaped domes of St. Basil's paste paper strips together (see illustration), or you might want to use papier-mâché (see p. 145) for the many decorative touches. A novel project would be to make your buildings out of baker's clay, painted in bright colors.

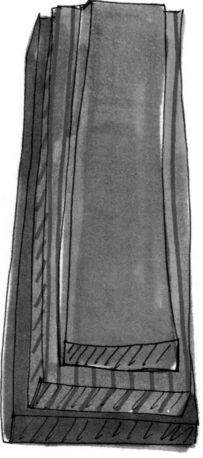

BAKER'S CLAY

YOU NEED: 4 cups (960 ml) flour
1 cup (240 ml) of salt
1½ cups (360 ml) water

YOU DO: 1. Mix all ingredients well, kneading until firm.

2. Working on a flat surface, use your fingers to form the shapes of the buildings. (A soft orangewood stick and dull table knife will be useful tools.)

3. Carefully place your completed buildings on a baking sheet and bake in a 350° F (180° C) oven about 30 minutes until light brown in color and firm to the touch.

Note: If you want to make your buildings three-dimensional, you will have to construct all four sides separately. Then after they are baked and painted, glue them together to form buildings.

Add rows of bushes and trees around the buildings, the permanent stands for parades in front of the Kremlin, and perhaps benches for the people to sit on in the warm weather.

May Day

Along the avenues reaching out from Red Square are large apartment buildings, many decorated with colorful mosaics or gigantic statues of laborers. Since the workers are considered the most important people of the Soviet Union, a special holiday, May Day, honors them. In Moscow there are parades that usually begin as small neighborhood groups, finally converging in Red Square in a colorful mass of flags and flowers. In Leningrad the focal point of the May Day celebration is the Winter Palace of the czars.

Easter

Many Christian holidays are also celebrated in the USSR with customs passed down from family to family. For example, on Easter, known as *Pashka,* a tall cake, or *koulich,* is traditionally eaten. The Russian initials *KV,* standing for the words "Khristos voskress" (Christ is risen), are often imprinted on the frosting.

KOULICH

YOU NEED:

a basic recipe or packaged white-cake mix and powdered-sugar icing

⅓ cup (80 ml) raisins

½ cup (120 ml) chopped candied fruits

2-pound coffee can

3 tablespoons (45 ml) chopped walnuts

vanilla

sprinkles: sugared confetti, candied fruits and silver dragées

YOU DO:

1. Mix cake according to directions, adding the raisins, chopped fruits, nuts and a dash of vanilla.

2. Pour batter into several round layer pans or into a 2-pound, *well-greased* coffee can. Bake in a 350° F (180° C) oven for 1 hour.

3. Let cool after baking; then spread icing over the top and add sprinkles.

Pysanky (Egg-decorating)

Ukrainians are particularly well-known for the beautiful folk art of *pysanky,* a craft passed down from generation to generation. Their implements are a *kistka,* a small writing instrument, a lighted candle, some shavings of beeswax and several jars of brilliant dyes. A finished design may take many hours and have a dozen layers of wax and dyes! The eggs are not cooked or blown out but eventually dry out when left uncovered.

You might experiment with a simpler batik-type process:

Hold a lighted birthday candle over the egg and drip some wax on it. (This will become the light part of your design.) Now dip the egg into some dye until it turns the shade you want. Add more wax, if you wish, and dip into a second color. You may leave the wax on, or soften it in a barely warm oven before rubbing it off with a cloth.

The many intricate designs of the Ukrainians are based on symbols. Wheat represents the bountiful harvest. (Since early times the Ukraine has been considered the "breadbasket of Europe.") Waves and ribbons circling an egg without a beginning or an end symbolize eternity. The fish, cross, triangle and eight-pointed star all have meanings closely associated with Christ. The colors have significance, too: red for love, pink for success, blue for health and yellow for spirituality. The eggs are given as Easter gifts but are proudly displayed year-round. (A ring cut from a cardboard tube and covered makes a perfect egg stand.)

New Year's

New Year's, rather than Christmas, is the highlight of the Soviet winter season and on that day you'll even find New Year's trees in Soviet homes. *Dyed Maroz,* Grandfather Frost, brings toys to "good boys and girls"; it is said that he comes from the far north and moves so quickly that no one ever sees him.

Birthdays

Of course, birthdays are special celebrations too. Your teacher might want to keep a record of each student's birthdate, as is done in the Soviet schools; then when a birthday is approaching, a committee can plan ways to celebrate the occasion. If you were the birthday girl, you would wear red, blue or green bows on your braids to set off your school uniform.

KARAVAI (THE ROUND LOAF)

Books and wooden toys are favorite birthday gifts and *Karavai* is a popular party game for children of all ages. Try it with your younger brothers and sisters, too. Hold hands and dance around the birthday child, chanting:

On Natasha's birthday we have a round loaf
So high (Raise joined hands over heads)
So low (Stoop down)
So wide (Make a circle as large as possible)
So narrow (Move in toward the center, making the
    circle smaller, and gently tap the birthday child)

The group gradually steps backward, chanting as they go: "Round Loaf, Round Loaf. Let him who wishes take some." The birthday child says: "I love you all but someone special more than all!" Choosing someone to take her place, the birthday child then joins the circle and the game continues.

You might want to bake a "birthday pie" as many Soviet children do. Use a toothpick to prick out the name of the "honored child" and the birthday greeting, *S Dnyem Rozh Denya,* on the crust before it is baked. Usually the pie is apple or cherry, and the birthday child gets the first piece.

A Soviet child's sixteenth birthday is an especially important one because he is now considered an adult and is given his own passport for traveling throughout the country. At eighteen he becomes a voter in the national elections.

Weddings

Weddings in the USSR are strictly civil ceremonies with a member of the city Soviet (council), often a woman, presiding. There are no religious vows, just an official explanation of love, respect, friendship and responsibility. The bride wears the traditional long white gown and flowered headpiece. In Leningrad the Palace of Weddings is open ten hours a day, seven days a week, and more than forty marriages are performed there each day. Often a newly married bride and groom will be descending the marble steps just as another couple is going up, a good example of Soviet efficiency. There is a minimum charge for the wedding itself, and for an extra fee, the government will provide flowers, photographs and a champagne reception.

CIRCUS

Everyone loves the circus and in the Soviet Union every big city has its own. In Moscow there are two — the old and new — and they are a particular treat for all of the villagers who come into the city for entertainment.

MINIATURE CIRCUS

Creating your own circus can turn into a colorful, imaginative project. Make a circus train procession of shoebox "cars" or open lids for flat-top "exhibits," or use the same materials for a three-dimensional group mural for the wall. Include paper or cardboard animals with fringed manes and tails. Be sure to feature a bear, as Soviet children particularly love their "Honey-Paw," the highlight of the circus and a symbol of good luck.

Cages for the animals can be made by gluing drinking straws or pieces of mesh potato or onion bags onto cardboard frames. Cardboard tubes and straws wrapped in foil make shiny poles and swings for the acrobat or trapeze acts. A tent can be constructed from paper bags or cloth scraps; transparent cellophane will allow the viewer to see the main show inside.

In the Soviet Union most performances are held indoors and a huge covered arena was recently built as a permanent home for the new Moscow State Circus. A special feature of all the Soviet circuses is the clowns, who, in their harlequin dress, act as masters of ceremonies. Karandash, the most famous of all, is known throughout the world.

A REAL CIRCUS

An ambitious project would be to convert your back-yard or school playground into a real circus with gymnasts, acrobatic acts and decorated "circus wagons" filled with all the neighborhood animals. Set up games of skill and chance, and recruit a barker, a balloon man and a juggler. From a push-cart or a kiosk (wooden booth) sell popcorn, pea-nuts, cola, lemonade, chocolate-coated ice cream on a stick, and cotton candy, all of which are favorites of Soviet circus audiences. A common scene at the Soviet circus is the pretzel vendor who wears stacks of huge pretzel bracelets up and down both arms.

PRETZELS

YOU NEED:
1 cake active, fresh yeast or 1 envelope dry yeast
1½ cups (360 ml) lukewarm
   (110°–115° F; 43°–46° C) water
¾ teaspoon (3¾ ml) salt
1½ teaspoons (7½ ml) sugar
4 cups (960 ml) flour
1 egg, beaten
coarse (kosher) salt

YOU DO:
1. In a large bowl dissolve the yeast in the water, then add the sugar and the salt.
2. Mix in the flour and knead until the dough is soft and smooth.
3. Do not let the dough rise; instead, divide immediately into smaller pieces and roll into ropes. Form the ropes into circles and pretzel shapes.
5. Place on a cookie sheet covered with foil and dusted with flour.
6. Brush each pretzel with the beaten egg mixed with a little water and sprinkle with coarse salt.
7. Bake in a 400° F (204° C) oven (about 10 minutes) until brown.

Note: These pretzels taste better when eaten warm.

SPACE

Soviet children are proud of their country's pioneering in space. Did you know that the Space Age began in 1957 when the Soviet's "Sputnik," meaning fellow traveler or satellite, was the first spaceship to circle the earth? It looked something like a ball of yarn with knitting needles through it, measuring twenty-two inches across and weighing a little over 183 pounds. Sputnik II, which followed, carried one passenger, a dog, Laika! It circled the earth ninety times and traveled 3,500,000 miles.

However, most people associate the beginning of the Space Age with the first *man* in space, Yuri Gagarin, who orbited the earth on April 21, 1961. His spaceship was called Vostok, the Russian word for East. Gagarin, as well as those who followed him (such as Gherman Titov, the team of Nikolayev and Popovich, and Valentina Tereshkova, the first woman in space), called themselves "cosmonauts," derived from two Greek words and meaning "sailors of the universe."

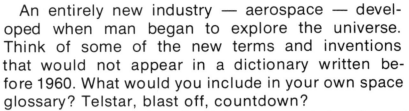

An entirely new industry — aerospace — developed when man began to explore the universe. Think of some of the new terms and inventions that would not appear in a dictionary written before 1960. What would you include in your own space glossary? Telstar, blast off, countdown?

Even the term "hot line" has entered the Space Age! Washington and Moscow are now able to teletype each other instantly via a communication satellite. Although there has been an underground hot line between these two cities since 1963, many mishaps have occurred, such as the accidental cutting of cables by a deep-sea fishing trawler and the plow of a Finnish farmer, as well as a fire in a Baltimore manhole! Now, with the new signals transmitted through space, these problems should be eliminated.

Combine math, science and geography in solving a telecommunications problem. How would you measure the distance between a major sports event (perhaps the 1980 Moscow Olympics), a communication satellite and your receiver (your own TV set)? How long would it take the picture signal to reach you? What purpose does the satellite serve?

Space Fantasy

If *you* are excited about the concept of space travel, you can imagine how your parents and grandparents must feel — they who only fantasized as children about the "man in the moon," "green cheese" and "Martians invading the earth." In July 1976 the U.S. Viking I, landing on Mars, found red, rocky soil . . . but no Martians.

To explore the age-old romantic notions of the moon and Mars in literature, you could make an illustrated book including all the poems, songs, nursery rhymes, stories and superstitions that you can find.

You might also plan a space flight and list the items needed for your journey — some space food, a flight suit, scientific instruments, even bolted-down furniture. Gagarin had a special camera that photographed more of the earth's surface than had ever been seen in one view. Perhaps you could bring along a camera for your flight!

SPORTS

Soviet children, just like their counterparts throughout the world, like to play hopscotch, checkers, volleyball, soccer and badminton. They enjoy rowing on the lake and riding the gigantic Ferris wheel in Gorki Park, one of eleven "parks of culture and rest" in Moscow that are open for recreation year-round. Although Soviet summers are short, swimming is a favorite pastime, especially on the beaches along the banks of the Moscow River, where young people gather to swim, picnic, sun, sing and play jazz on their guitars. The Moscow River is also the scene of winter activity, serving as an icy landing place for skiers zooming down from the snowy Lenin Hills. Another amazing sight in winter is the huge *outdoor* heated swimming pool in Moscow where hundreds of people can be seen splashing, even in below-zero weather or during a snowstorm!

Soccer and hockey are the most important sports. The government spends a great deal of money on athletics, building thousands of stadiums and playing fields (the huge Lenin Stadium in Moscow seats more than one hundred thousand people), and sponsoring large sports festivals. The Soviet Union's emphasis on training and discipline in athletics also carries over to the schools where calisthenics and games to promote physical fitness are required after-school activities.

Olympics

Soviet athletes, known to be tops in their field, took home the most medals (a total of 125), in the 1976 summer Olympics. They won 47 gold, 43 silver and 35 bronze medals, in such divisions as track, wrestling, judo, handball, gymnastics, weightlifting, fencing and cycling.

Plan a summer or winter Olympics for your school or neighborhood. What events would you feature? Be sure to provide banners for each team and medals and ribbons for the winners.

CHESS

The Soviets are considered the best chess players in the world, learning the game at a very early age. Of the fifteen chess titlists who have won the world record since its beginnings in 1866, eight have been from the Soviet Union. Most recently, Boris Spassky held the title from 1969 to 1972 and Anatoly Karpov won the championship in 1975.

CHESS SET
Although you can buy an inexpensive chess set (*sháchmati*), making your own would be a creative project. Just for the fun of it, you might substitute czars for the kings and peasants for the pawns. For your chess pieces you can use wooden spools, dowel rods cut into various lengths or even wooden clothes-pins stuck in a clay base. Glue wooden beads to the top, decorate and then shellac, if you wish. "Parquet" pieces can be made by gluing chunks of wood together and then staining them. Make your chess-board from plywood that you've sanded and stained or paste squares of contact paper or heavy fabric onto a masonite or plywood base. You could also make a *giant* chessboard using glued-together carpet samples. Two teams of very patient children could be the chessmen, or perhaps you would prefer to use graduated sizes of empty tin cans!

GAMES

The Soviets like to play a game called "Czar and Peasants." The czar stands before his subjects, dressed in rich robes, and inquires, "Well, subjects, what have you been doing?" The peasants perform a pantomime that they have agreed to present to the czar, and if he guesses what they're doing, they run to the goal line trying not to be tagged. Whoever is tagged becomes the next czar!

Other popular tag games in Russia are "The Bear" and "The Gypsy." In "The Gypsy," the players dance around in a circle, slowly chanting, while the gypsy, standing in the center, pantomimes their words: "The first hour the gypsy is asleep, the second hour the gypsy is asleep, the third . . . the fourth . . . the fifth hour the gypsy gets up, the sixth hour the gypsy dresses, the seventh hour the gypsy washes, the eighth hour the gypsy gets ready . . . the twelfth, the gypsy runs!" At the word "runs," the players drop hands and run in all directions trying *not* to be tagged. The player who gets caught becomes the next gypsy.

"The Bear" is a variation of chain tag; when "it" tags someone, the two join hands and chant "the Bear is coming"; they then try to tag somebody else with their free hands. Incidentally, the bear still roams freely in the sparsely populated woodlands of the north, and a great deal of mythology and many superstitions as well as games have developed around him.

WOODEN TOYS AND BOXES

Simple unpainted toys are very popular in the Soviet Union and young children especially treasure their hand-carved *medvid* (bear). Since every child is trained early in life to be a good citizen, it is not surprising that many Soviet toys are miniature copies of real life — sturdy wooden replicas of trucks, steam shovels, trains, cradles, simple furniture, household objects, school desks and of course, dolls. Through the dolls children practice the roles they might assume in adulthood. Therefore, there are doll doctors, nurses, teachers, workers, even students dressed in school uniforms, complete with the red handkerchiefs of the Young Pioneers.

You might enjoy making a set of "real life" dolls using cardboard or heavy construction paper. If you glue felt onto the doll's body, you can then create felt clothes that will stick directly to the doll; paper clothes with a bit of felt glued to the back will also stay on the doll.

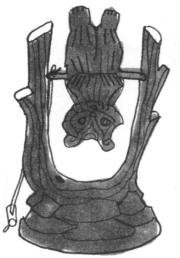

Matryoshka (Dolls)

A favorite toy of Soviet children is the colorful *matryoshka* stacking dolls. Although they are generally made of brightly painted wood, you can make yours out of papier-mâché, or use three different-sized tin cans, margarine tubs, spray can lids or paper cups that *nest* inside each other. For a peasant look, paint a face on each one, add hair, a *babushka* tied around the head, and a floral-patterned apron or pinafore over a dark dress. Some *matryoshka* are made up of as many as twenty nesting dolls, the tiniest one being a wooden bead with room for only the eyes.

Lacquered Boxes

Because wood is so plentiful in the Soviet Union, it is used not only for the decorative stacking dolls, but also for the even more intricately designed *shkatulki,* the beautiful lacquered boxes prized throughout the world.

To create imitation *shkatulki,* collect a variety of cardboard boxes and lids. Paint designs on the outside or cover them with cutout pictures before adding several coats of shellac for a highly polished surface. The boxes are usually decorated in rich oranges, reds, golds and blues on a jet-black background, and lined in a brilliant red. The authentic ones in the Soviet Union have miniature pictures from folktales or ancient legends; common designs are the "Firebird" with its brightly colored feathers, the "Magic Carpet," or the "Troika," the traditional Russian three-horse team.

SHELLAC

BALLET

The Soviet Union takes special pride in the ballet. Today approximately thirty-two cities have their own ballet troupes. Even the remotest areas enjoy performances by traveling companies. Coming to this art relatively late, Russians learned ballet in the 1700s, primarily from established French and Italian dancers, but then surpassed even their teachers in many ways. Toward the end of the century Russia's two Imperial Schools of Ballet were founded, first the "Bolshoi" (great) Theater in Moscow, and then the "Bolshoi" in St. Petersburg (renamed Leningrad after the Revolution), which later became the Kirov State Ballet.

These two outstanding ballet theaters, even today, reflect the differences in style of the two cities. For example, in St. Petersburg, "the city of the royal court," classical ballet with its strict patterns was perfected for the czars. Anna Pavlova (famed for her role as the "Dying Swan") and Waslaw Nijinsky were both products of this traditional school. (Did you know that George Balanchine, the well-known American choreographer, was born in Russia and trained at the Imperial School at St. Petersburg?)

In contrast to St. Petersburg, Moscow was considered a "peasant city" without the same degree of culture. The Moscow School emphasized the dramatic "tours de force," vigorous athletic stunts and endurance. Ulanova, the most spirited member of this Bolshoi, became a symbol of the "greatness of Soviet ballet."

The genius of Serge Diaghilev made Russia the leader of the ballet world from 1885 to 1914. This great impresario, who founded the Ballet Russe, broke out of the classical mold, combining drama, music, color and choreography to make ballet a total art form. The virile, leaping "Polovetsian Dances" from *Prince Igor* and the exotic costume designs of *Scheherazade* are two examples of his contemporary approach. You might enjoy learning about several ballets — both classical and modern, and compare them as to mood, style and content. Perhaps you could start with Peter Tchaikovsky's music for three enchanting ballets — *Swan Lake, The Sleeping Beauty* and *The Nutcracker.*

The Nutcracker

The Nutcracker Suite, often referred to as the Christmas or Children's Ballet, has become the most popular holiday stage spectacle in the United States. Read the story first, then close your eyes and listen to the music . . . you will probably "see" the Stahlbaum family putting the finishing touches on their huge Christmas tree and the Sugar Plum Fairy and Nutcracker himself spring to life, along with such delights as Hot Chocolate (depicted by a group of Spanish dancers), Coffee (a moody Arab accompanied by four huge parrots) and Tea (a Chinese man).

Cinderella

The composer Sergei Prokofiev chose the story of Cinderella for a ballet and his music helps the listener visualize the familiar scenes. As you listen to the orchestra, you will recognize the ugly sisters teasing Cinderella, the appearance of the fairy godmother, the elegant ball where Cinderella dances with the prince, and so on. Prokofiev, a child prodigy, was composing his own music before he was six years old! (He also wrote the musical fairy tale, *Peter and the Wolf,* in which Peter, Grandfather and Peter's friends, the duck, cat and bird, speak in musical voices.) It might be fun to pantomime the actions of the characters in the *Nutcracker Suite* and *Cinderella* at the appropriate points in the music . . . simple props and costumes could also be used.

Why do you think Tchaikovsky and Prokofiev used these particular stories for ballets? If you were to write a ballet, what stories would you choose?

Moisheyev Dancers

When you think about Russia's great contribution to the art of dance, of course Igor Moisheyev's exciting dance company comes to mind! It is said that since 1937 Moisheyev has furnished the world with the finest example of contemporary Soviet choreography. He is noted for his large troupes of colorful dancers from various republics all over Russia performing their own regional dances. Their steps vary from simple peasant rhythms to the most sensational leaps and stunts ever witnessed in the theater. There is a feeling of magic and vitality in all of his work!

FOOD

The custom of eating "family style," with platters full of food passed around the table, started in Russia. The meals are long and filling, beginning with appetizers such as herring or other fish (caviar has become so rare that it is now used for export only), then progressing to soup, meat, potatoes and vegetables. Dessert and tea without flavoring complete the meal.

Probably the most typical soups are beet *borscht* and cabbage *borscht,* which are always served with sour cream.

CABBAGE BORSCHT

YOU NEED:
- ¼ cup (60 ml) vegetable oil
- 1 tablespoon (15 ml) flour
- 1 large onion, chopped
- 2 quarts (1.9 L) water
- 8-ounce (226.8-gram) can tomato sauce
- 1 tablespoon (15 ml) salt
- 1½ pounds (680.4 grams) chopped raw cabbage
- 2 large beets, cubed peppercorns
- 1 bay leaf
- 2 large carrots, cubed
- 1 green pepper, chopped (optional)

YOU DO:
1. Sauté onion in oil, stirring in flour and then water until mixed well.
2. Add remaining ingredients and simmer over low heat for about 1 hour.
3. Be sure to taste the *borscht* to see if it needs more spice or perhaps a little sugar. Serves 6 to 8.

If you attended a Soviet school, your lunch would probably consist of soup, brown bread and a cup of hot chocolate . . . and you would be asked to sit until you finished your entire meal.

Because of the lack of refrigeration and storage space, the parent, or perhaps the grandmother, the *babushka,* goes out early each morning to get fresh milk. She stands in long lines clutching her *avosica* (mesh shopping bag), which soon will be bulging with fresh bread, vegetables and fruit brought swiftly from the provinces by river hydrofoils. Waiting in line is as much a part of daily living in the Soviet Union as going to work or attending school. If there is a "special," it is necessary to get in line even earlier, sometimes only to find that the supply is exhausted by the time it's your turn. There's a basic rule of thumb that if you see something for sale that you like, buy it, because tomorrow it probably won't be there!

Most shops in Moscow can be identified by number instead of by name, such as Gastronom No. 5 (food shop), Stolovia No. 15 (cafeteria) or Apteka No. 8 (pharmacy). All items for sale are selected by the state, so most stores have identical products at the same prices, eliminating any competition. At a Stolovia, bread is not sold by the slice, but by the gram. The cafeteria server carefully weighs each piece so that no one gets slightly more or less than his two kopecks' worth. Very few stores have cash registers; instead clerks use wooden abacuses. Sometimes the customer gets his change in postage stamps, or even in matches if small change runs short. For instance, ice cream is 19 kopecks and if you give a 20-kopeck coin, you're likely to get back one box of matches!

Since both parents work all day, there are many *Kulinarias* (delicatessens) that sell partly cooked dishes, especially casseroles that can be quickly heated at home.

SOLYANKA (SAUERKRAUT)

YOU NEED:

¼ cup (60 ml) cooking oil
1 large onion, chopped
1 large can of sauerkraut (approximately 1½ pounds — 680.4 grams — rinsed in hot water and squeezed dry)
1 medium carrot, shredded
1 apple, shredded
1 teaspoon (5 ml) salt
¼ cup (60 ml) sugar
½ teaspoon (2½ ml) caraway seeds
1 teaspoon (5 ml) ground pepper
¼ cup (60 ml) water
2 strips of bacon, uncooked
1 pound (453.6 grams) cooked ham, cubed

YOU DO:

1. Fry onion in oil, adding sauerkraut, shredded carrot and apple, salt, sugar, caraway seeds, ground pepper and water.
2. Mix well and place in large casserole, laying strips of bacon on top.
3. Bake at 350° F (180° C) for about 1½ hours.
4. 15 minutes before the *Solyanka* is done, add the cooked ham. Serves 6 to 8.

LUKSHENA KÜGEL (NOODLE PUDDING)

YOU NEED:

½ pound (226.8 grams) medium noodles
4 tablespoons (60 ml) margarine
3 eggs, beaten
1¼ teaspoon (1.25 ml) salt
1 cup (240 ml) cottage cheese

YOU DO:

1. Cook noodles in 2 quarts (1.9 L) boiling salted water until tender.
2. Drain and stir in margarine, eggs, salt and cottage cheese.
3. Pour into a greased 8 x 8 inch (20.3 x 20.3 cm) pan and bake at 375° F (190° C) for 50 minutes or until golden brown.

In the Ukraine this *kügel* is served with a glass of hot tea flavored with jam or a slice of apple. Some cooks like to incorporate raisins, apricots, sour cream and cinnamon into their *kügel* recipe.

Sirniki are a popular dessert—pancakes small enough to pick up and eat in one bite. They, too, are served the "Russian" way with sour cream.

SIRNIKI

YOU NEED:
- 2 eggs
- ½ cup (120 ml) cream cheese (softened)
- 1 tablespoon (15 ml) sugar
- ½ teaspoon (2½ ml) salt
- 1 cup (240 ml) cottage cheese
- ½ cup (120 ml) flour
- 4 tablespoons (60 ml) margarine or butter

YOU DO:
1. Separate 2 eggs and mix the yolks with the softened cream cheese, sugar and salt.
2. Stir in cottage cheese and add sifted flour. Mix until the batter is smooth.
3. Beat egg whites until stiff and then fold into the batter.
4. Heat 2 tablespoons (30 ml) of butter at a time in a frying pan until it sizzles, and drop the batter by heaping tablespoons into the pan to form pancakes.

Cream cheese is also an important ingredient in the following flavorful tarts.

VATRUSHKY (CHEESE TARTS)

YOU NEED:

Cream Cheese Pastry:
1 cup + 2 tablespoons (240 ml + 30 ml) unbleached flour
¾ teaspoon (3¾ ml) salt
4 tablespoons (60 ml) butter
1 3-ounce (85 grams) package cream cheese
1 egg, beaten

Filling:
6 ounces (170 grams) cream cheese
3 tablespoons (45 ml) sour cream
1 teaspoon (5 ml) sugar
¼ teaspoon (1¼ ml) salt
¼ teaspoon (1¼ ml) freshly grated lemon peel
¼ cup (60 ml) currants

YOU DO:

1. Sift together flour and salt and then cut in the butter and cream cheese.
2. Add egg and mix well.
3. Roll pastry ⅛ inch thick and then cut into 3-inch rounds and press into small muffin tins.
4. Combine all the ingredients for the filling and spoon into the pastry.
5. Bake for 20 minutes at 375° F (190° C), until edges are golden brown.

Gogel-Mogel also tastes delicious when spooned over vanilla pudding or ice cream.

GOGEL-MOGEL

Russian children have always loved this simple but rich golden dessert, particularly on special treat days, birthdays and festivals. The name conjures up pictures of legendary folk creatures — fairies, gnomes and enchanted animals enjoying this golden syrup while having snowy picnics in the deep forest of the Ukraine.

YOU NEED:
4 egg yolks
6 tablespoons (90 ml) light-brown sugar
¼ teaspoon (1¼ ml) vanilla (optional)

YOU DO:

1. Mix the egg yolks, brown sugar and vanilla together, beating the mixture until it becomes thick and smooth.
2. Pour into custard glasses and eat.

THE SOVIET UNION LANGUAGE

The Russian language is written in the Cyrillic alphabet. It is much like the language of other Slavic countries (Poland, Yugoslavia, etc.), although its pronunciation differs. An example of Cyrillic is **МОЙ ДРУГ** (my friend), which is pronounced "moi droog."

PRONUNCIATION TIPS

The following words are spelled out phonetically in English letters. The vowel "i" usually has the sound of "$\overline{ee}$" (blini = bleenee). Double and triple consonants are used to approximate the guttural sounds of the Russian language. (The sounds fst, zd, tz, sht, as well as others, are actually represented by one letter in the Cyrillic alphabet.)

COMMON EXPRESSIONS

Hello	Zdrásdvitche	How are you?	Kak vi paziv(y)iti?
Good morning	Dóbroye utra	Good night	Dóbra viecher
Please	Pajálsta	Thank you	Spaéeba
I love you	Ya vas looblue	Good-bye	Dósvedania

What is your name?	Kak vas zavout?
My name is _____.	Menyá zavut _____.
How old are you?	Skolka vam liet?
I am _____ years old.	Mniye _____ liet.

Numbers

1 adín	4 chítiri	7 siém	10 diéset
2 dua	5 piát	8 vóisim	11 odínatzat
3 tree	6 shest	9 diévet	12 dvenádtzat

This is my _____.

mother	mat
father	dzadzie
brother	brat

Eto (male) eta (female) _____.

sister	sistrá
teacher	oóchitiel
friend	droog

INTERNATIONAL POTPOURRI

There are many ways to bring together and highlight the special features of the six countries in this book (or of any country you might be studying). Events such as a craft bazaar, trade fair, ethnic dinner or a music and dance festival will provide ideal themes to further international understanding.

An *international menu* like this one combines food specialties from every part of the globe . . . truly a taster's delight!

**AROUND THE WORLD
MENU**

Nigerian Ground Nut Soup
Shah's Salad from Iran
Japanese Chicken Teriyaki
Lukshena Kügel from the Soviet Union
A Brazilian coconut drink, Refresco de Coco
Petit Fours and other desserts from the French Patisserie

Other Ideas to Try

WORLDWIDE BAZAAR

Bring your francs, kopeks and yen to shop for the many hand-crafted items filling the colorful stalls.

MINI-UN

Assemble delegates from each country to debate current issues, such as foreign affairs, health and nutrition, boundary disputes, economic problems, and so on.

INTERNATIONAL FRIENDSHIP DAY

Plan a special day when everyone can actively participate in projects that will lead to a better understanding and appreciation of other cultures. Present a play or puppet show depicting scenes from historical or contemporary life; take part in a fashion show with typical costumes of various countries; compete in an international Olympics with games and athletic contests; join in folk singing and dancing . . . or feature a holiday celebration or parade to highlight the customs and traditions of children around the world.

BIBLIOGRAPHY

GENERAL

CBS News Almanac. New Jersey: Hammond Almanac, Inc., 1977.

Comptons Encyclopedia. Chicago: University of Chicago Press, 1973.

Cobb, Vicki. *Science Experiments You Can Eat.* Philadelphia: J. B. Lippincott Co., 1972.

Craig, Gerald. *Science for the Elementary School Teacher.* Lexington, Mass.: Ginn & Co., 1958.

Instructor magazine (Dansville, New York: Instructor Publication, Inc.): Brazil, November 1976; Iran, May 1977; Nigeria, October 1976.

Jones, Robert M. *Can Elephants Swim?* New York: Time, Inc., 1969.

Joseph, Joan. *Folk Toys Around the World.* New York: Parents' Magazine Press, 1972.

National Geographic: Japan, May 1972; September 1972; March 1974; June 1976
  Nigeria, August 1975
  Soviet Union, March 1966; May 1971; April 1972
  Brazil, July 1961; January 1966; October 1972; November 1977
  Iran, January 1975

United States Committee for UNICEF (ed.). *Hi Neighbor* Series. New York: United Nations.

United States Committee for UNICEF (ed.). *Sing, Children, Sing.* New York: Quadrangle, 1973.

World Almanac. New York: Newspaper Enterprise Association, Inc., 1977.

World Book Encyclopedia. Chicago: Field Enterprises, Inc., 1975.

COOKING

Beard, James. "A Quiche is a Quiche, Not a Tart," *Chicago Daily News,* November 6, 1976.

Berry, Erick. *Eating and Cooking Around the World.* New York: John Day Co., 1963.

Blanch, Lesley. *Around the World in Eighty Dishes.* New York: Harper & Bros., 1955.

Castle, Coralie, and Gin, Margaret. *Country Cookery, Recipes of Many Lands.* San Francisco: 101 Productions, 1975.

Chang, Constance D. *The Japanese Menu Cookbook.* New York: Doubleday & Co., 1976.

Child, Julia, et al. *Mastering the Art of French Cooking,* Vols. I and II. New York: Alfred A. Knopf, 1961, 1973.

Cooper, Terry Touff, and Ratner, Marilyn. *Many Hands Cooking.* New York: T. Y. Crowell Co., 1974.

Lucas, Christopher. "The Heavenly Food of Japan," *Reader's Digest,* May 1977.

Lucas, Dione, *The Cordon Bleu Cook Book.* Boston, Mass.: Little, Brown & Co., 1947.

Mazda, Maideh. *In a Persian Kitchen.* Rutland, Vt.: Charles E. Tuttle, 1975.

Mendes, Helen. *The African Heritage Cookbook.* New York: Macmillan Co., 1970.

Metzelthin, Pearl V. *The New World Wide Cookbook.* New York: Julian Messner, Inc., 1951.

Oka, M. Odinchezo. *Black Academy Cookbook.* Buffalo, N.Y.: Black Academy Press, Inc., 1972.

Shapiro, Rebecca. *A Whole World of Cooking.* Boston, Mass.: Little, Brown & Co., 1972.

Ward, Artemus. *Encyclopedia of Food.* Gloucester, Mass.: Peter Smith, 1971.

Weppner, Eileen. *The International Grandmothers' Cookbook.* Boulder, Colo.: Blue Mountain Arts, Inc., 1974.

Zane, Eva. *Middle Eastern Cookery.* San Francisco: 101 Productions, 1974.

GAMES

Arnold, Arnold. *The World Book of Children's Games.* New York: World Publishing Co., 1972.

Grunfeld, Frederic V. *Games of the World.* New York: Holt, Rinehart & Winston, 1975.

Harbin, E. O. *Games of Many Nations.* New York: Abingdon Press, 1954.

Hunt, Sarah Ethridge, and Cain, Ethel. *Games the World Around.* New York: Barnes & Co., 1950.

McWhirter, Mary Esther. *Games Enjoyed by Children Around the World.* Philadelphia: American Friends Service Committee, 1970.

Millen, Nina. *Children's Games from Many Lands.* New York: Friendship Press, 1965.

HOLIDAYS

Dobler, Lavinia. *Customs and Holidays Around the World.* New York: Fleet Press Corp., 1962.

————————. *National Holidays Around the World.* New York: Fleet Press Corp., 1968.

Johnson, Lois S. *Happy Birthdays Round the World.* Chicago: Rand McNally & Co., 1963.

————————. *Happy New Year Round the World.* Chicago: Rand McNally & Co., 1963.

Manning-Sanders, Ruth, comp. *Festivals.* New York: E. P. Dutton & Co., 1973.

Spiegelman, Judith. *UNICEF's Festival Book.* New York: U.S. Committee for UNICEF, 1966.

BRAZIL

Breetveld, James. *Getting to Know Brazil.* New York: Coward-McCann, Inc., 1960.

Brown, Rose. *The Land and People of Brazil.* Philadelphia: J. B. Lippincott Co., 1972.

Carpenter, Allan. *Brazil* (Enchantment of South America Series). Chicago: Childrens Press, 1968.

Dutton, E. P. (ed.), *The Voyage of the Beagle.* New York: E. P. Dutton & Co., 1976.

Fideler, Raymond, and Kvande, Carol. *South America.* Grand Rapids, Mich.: The Fideler Co., 1964.

May, Stella Burke. *Brazil.* Grand Rapids, Mich.: The Fideler Co., 1967.

Morgan, Ted. "Brazil," *Travel and Leisure Magazine.* New York: U.S. Camera Publishing Corp., October 1975.

Robock, Stefan. "Realizing the Miracle," *Saturday Review,* Oct. 18, 1976.

Sheppard, Sally. *The First Book of Brazil.* New York: Franklin Watts, Inc., 1972.

Sutton, Horace. "Flying Down to Rio," *Saturday Review,* Oct. 18, 1976.

FRANCE

Baird, Bil. *The Art of the Puppet.* Verona, Italy: copyright Ridge Press, Inc., 1973.

Black, J. Anderson, and Garland, Madge. *A History of Fashion.* New York: William Morrow & Co., 1975.

Bragdon, Lillian. *The Land and People of France.* Philadelphia: J. B. Lippincott Co., 1960.

Edwards, Harvey. *France and the French.* New York: Thomas Nelson, 1972.

Garland, Madge. *The Changing Form of Fashion.* New York: Praeger Publishers, 1971.

Harris, Leon A. *Young France.* New York: Dodd, Mead & Co., 1964.

"Perfume is Social Dynamite in an Expensive Package," *Smithsonian,* Washington, D.C.: Smithsonian Institution, February 1976.

ART

Chelminski, Rudolph. "Exoskeletal Art Container is the Rage, Literally, and the Delight of Paris," *Smithsonian,* Washington, D.C.: Smithsonian Institution, August 1977.

Hunter, Sam. *Modern French Painting.* New York: Dell Publishing Co., 1956.

Kay-Robinson, Denys. *Adverturing with Art.* Feltham, Middlesex, England: Kay-Robinson Odhams Books, Hamlyn Publishing Group, 1968.

Pocket Books (ed.). *Pocket Library of Great Art.* New York: Harry N. Abrams, Inc., 1954.

IRAN

Bahar, Hushang. *Getting to Know Iran and Iraq.* New York: Coward-McCann, Inc., 1963.

Bateson, Mary Catherine. *At Home in Iran.* Tehran, Iran: St. Pauls Church, 1976.

Hinckley, Helen. *The Land and People of Iran.* Philadelphia: J. B. Lippincott Co., 1973.

Hurean, Jean. *Iran Today.* Holland: Jeune Afrique Editions, 1975.

Lengyel, Emil. *Iran.* New York: Franklin Watts, Inc. 1972.

Liebetrau, Preben. *Oriental Rugs in Colour.* New York: Macmillan Co., 1963.

Lovejoy, Bahija. *Other Bible Lands.* New York: Abingdon Press, 1961.

Tattersall, C. E. C. *Notes on Carpet Knotting and Weaving.* London, England: Victoria and Albert Museum — Her Majesty's Stationery Office, 1969.

JAPAN

Buell, Hal. *Festivals of Japan.* New York: Dodd, Mead & Co., 1965.

Dearmin, Jennie T., and Peck, H. E. *Japan, Home of the Sun.* San Francisco: Harr Wagner Publishing, 1963.

Elliott, Lawrence. "Made in Japan: The World's Longest Railway Tunnel," *Reader's Digest,* September 1976.

Henderson, Ruby. *Visiting Japan.* Winnetka, Ill.: Board of Education, 1966.

Kaula, Edna Mason. *Japan Old and New.* New York: World Publishing Co., 1970.

Keene, Donald. *Bunraku, The Art of Japanese Puppet Theater.* Japan: Kodansha International Ltd., 1975.

Kirk, Ruth. *Japan: Crossroads of East and West.* Camden, N.J.: Thomas Nelson & Sons, 1966.

Seidensticker, Edward. *Japan.* New York: Time-Life Books, 1968.

Spencer, Cornelia (pseud.). *Made in Japan.* New York: Alfred A. Knopf, 1963.

Steinberg, Rafael. *Japan.* London, England: Collier-Macmillan Ltd., 1969.

Storry, Richard. *Countries of Today — Japan.* New York: David White, 1969.

NIGERIA

African Outreach Program (ed.). *African Children's Games for American Children.* Urbana-Champagne, Ill.: University of Illinois, 1975.

D'Amato, Janet and Alex. *African Crafts for You to Make.* New York: Julian Messner, 1969.

Dietz, Elisabeth and Olatunji, Michael Babatunde. *Musical Instruments of Africa.* New York: John Day Co., 1965.

Forman, Brenda-Lu and Harrison. *The Land and People of Nigeria.* Philadelphia: J. B. Lippincott Co., 1964.

Kittler, Glen D. *Let's Travel in Nigeria and Ghana.* Chicago: Childrens Press, 1965.

Spicer, E. *Peoples of Nigeria.* Nigeria: Longmans, 1962.

Standifer, James A., and Reeder, Barbara. *African and Afro-American Materials for Music Educators.* Reston, Va.: Music Educators National Conference, 1972.

AFRICAN FOLKTALES

Arnott, Kathleen. *African Myths and Legends.* New York: Henry Z. Walck, Inc., 1963.
Courlander, Harold. *The King's Drum and Other African Stories.* New York: Harcourt, Brace and World, Inc., 1962.
Courlander, Harold, and Herzog, George. *The Cow-Tail Switch and Other West African Stories.* New York: Henry Holt and Co., 1947.

SOVIET UNION

Gregory, Jane. "Magic of Ukrainian Eggs," *Chicago Sun-Times,* April 7, 1977.
Gunther, John. *Meet Soviet Russia.* Books I and II. New York: Harper & Row, 1962.
Jackson, W. A. Douglas. *Soviet Union.* Grand Rapids, Mich.: The Fideler Co., 1966.
Miller, Jack. *Life in Russia Today.* New York: G. P. Putnam's Sons, 1969.
"Russia's 60 Years of Communism — Success or Failure?" *U.S. News & World Report,* October 24, 1977.
Vandivert, Rita and William. *Young Russia.* New York: Dodd, Mead and Co., 1960.
Wallace, John A. *Getting to Know the Soviet Union.* New York: Coward-McCann, 1964.
Watson, Jane Werner. *The Soviet Union — Land of Many Peoples.* Champaign, Ill.: Garrard Publishing Co., 1973.

BALLET

Clarke, Mary, and Crisp, Clement. *Ballet: An Illustrated History.* New York: Universe Books, 1973.
DeMille, Agnes. *The Book of Dance.* New York: Golden Press, 1963.
Kerensky, Oleg. *The World of Ballet.* New York: Coward-McCann, 1970.
Maynard, Olga. *The Ballet Companion.* Philadelphia: MacRae Smith Co., 1957.